THE FUTURE OF INVESTMENT MANAGEMENT

Ronald N. Kahn

Statement of Purpose

The CFA Institute Research Foundation is a not-for-profit organization established to promote the development and dissemination of relevant research for investment practitioners worldwide.

Biography

Ronald N. Kahn is a managing director and global head of systematic equity research at BlackRock, where he has overall responsibility for the research underpinning the Systematic Active Equity products. His service with the firm dates back to 1998, including his years with Barclays Global Investors, which merged with BlackRock in 2009. Prior to that, he worked as director of research at Barra. An expert on portfolio management, risk modeling, and quantitative investing, Dr. Kahn has published numerous articles on investment management, and he coauthored, with Richard Grinold, *Active Portfolio Management: Quantitative Theory and Applications*. The two of them won the 2013 James R. Vertin award, presented periodically by CFA Institute to recognize individuals who have produced a body of research notable for its relevance and enduring value to investment professionals. He has won the Bernstein Fabozzi/Jacobs Levy award for best article in the *Journal of Portfolio Management*. Dr. Kahn is on the editorial advisory boards of the *Financial Analysts Journal*, the *Journal of Portfolio Management*, and the *Journal of Investment Consulting*. He teaches "International Equity and Currency Markets" in the Master of Financial Engineering Program at the University of California, Berkeley. Dr. Kahn received an AB in Physics, *summa cum laude*, from Princeton University and a PhD in Physics from Harvard University. He was a postdoctoral fellow in physics at the University of California, Berkeley.

Dedication

To another arc of history—from my parents, Ernest and Gloria Kahn, to my children, Max, Eli, and Katie. The future belongs to them.

26 May 2018

Contents

CE Qualified Activity ✷ **CFA Institute**   This publication qualifies for 4 CE credits under the guidelines of the CFA Institute Continuing Education Program.

Foreword

When an industry changes, it is essential to distinguish between core truths that will persist and traditional practice that may not endure. The institutional investment industry has been changing at a sedate pace since dawn of modern financial theory in the 1960s. Most of this change has occurred in the institutional investor sphere. However, the rate of change, amplified by technology, is starting to pick up and is increasingly causing a long-needed change in retail investing. Individual investors are becoming cost conscious and accepting of passive investment vehicles and other low-cost, highly diversified exchange-traded funds. It is gratifying to see the behemoths of retail investing battling it out in advertisements, each claiming the lowest prices.

Ron Kahn is perfectly positioned to be your guide through this transition. He has been an investment industry professional for more than 30 years. He is adept at theory and practice and, as a lecturer in finance at the University of California, Berkeley, Haas School of Business, he is familiar with the latest academic research. There is no better guide through this era of institutional transformation. This book is not the first time Ron has studied a transition. He earned his PhD at Harvard University with a thesis on the Big Bang, the prime transition. He worked with Luis Alvarez at Berkeley on another cataclysmic transition, nailing down the link between an asteroid impact and the extinction of the dinosaurs.

I had a boyhood friend who could take his India ink pen and, with five or six lines on paper, produce a recognizable image. How did he do it? Five lines, yet you knew who it was and what he was doing. Ron writes in this fashion. He can take a complicated subject and, in a couple of brief paragraphs, extract its essence. Ron's skill is in evidence in Chapters 2 and 3, which provide the historical backdrop to the current era.

Ron abides by the time-tested *rule of seven* as an organizing principle. We have seven seals, seven wonders of the world, seven deadly sins—even seven dwarfs and seven faculty rules at Monty Python's fictional University of Woolloomooloo. Why not seven insights into active management and seven trends in investment management? Ron uses the rule of seven to great effect.

The seventh insight into active management, regarding cost and constraints, is particularly relevant. Active managers strive to have good forecasts, but they are in something very close to a zero-sum game. Perfection is not expected or possible. In dealing with costs and constraints, there is no excuse for sloppy implementation. Poor estimation of transaction costs and slipshod trading are a substantial drain. Any constraint on a portfolio that is not mandated should be viewed as an admission that the drivers of the portfolio, the forecasts, and the portfolio construction process are poorly designed.

Of the seven trends in active management, the fourth—the big data theme—seems to be the most revolutionary. Can you afford to ignore it, and if you are a small shop, can you afford it at all? Ron does an excellent job laying out the scope of the big data challenge. One can only be sure that technological momentum will take us from the age of big data to the age of bigger data, so don't be left behind.

If you are studying for an MBA, preparing for your CFA Program exam, or a veteran investor who needs to prepare for the mid 21st century, then you will find this book an invaluable guide. It will provide a clear explanation of these crucial topics and point the way for anyone who wants to delve deeper.

Richard C. Grinold

Preface

This book grew out of two efforts that started in 2015. First, my group at BlackRock—the Systematic Active Equity team—held an investor symposium for our clients in May of that year. Raffaele Savi and Jeff Shen, the co-heads of the group, encouraged me to present a talk on the future of investment management. The winds of change had grown sufficiently strong that a talk on the general topic seemed appropriate. Soon after the symposium, I was delighted to receive an invitation to present the 2016 Thys Visser Commemorative Lecture Series at Stellenbosch University in South Africa. I chose to speak on the same topic, and the opportunity to present three hours of lectures allowed me to expand and more fully develop the material. The first version of this book, therefore, saw the light of day in South Africa. With those initial efforts behind me, I was quite receptive to discussions with Larry Siegel of the CFA Institute Research Foundation that led directly to this book.

Although the future of investment management is a big topic, a central arc traces through its history, and its trajectory predicts what will come in the next 5–10 years. Investment management is becoming increasingly *systematic*. Systems, analysis, structure, and understanding—built on increasingly available data—are replacing gut feelings and whims.

I participated in some of these developments over the past 30-plus years. When I entered finance, almost all investing was active investing. Index funds were relatively small. They had only begun generating profits for Wells Fargo Investment Advisors in 1984, a full 13 years after the firm developed and launched the first index fund product. Quantitative investing was in its infancy. Exchange-traded funds, so popular today, didn't appear until 1993. Investment data at that time were mainly fundamental and highly structured—for example, accounting statements and regulatory filings. Price and volume data were often analyzed at a monthly frequency, especially to understand risk and general trends.

Technology has advanced rapidly since 1987. At that time, one gigabyte of memory cost about $10,000. In 2018, it costs less than three cents. Popular 3.5-inch floppy disks stored 2.88 megabytes of data; several of them would be required to store one digital photo taken today. The internet didn't exist in 1987, though e-mail would become widely popular by the mid- to late 1990s. Today we have the internet, big data, and machine learning.

My career has focused on quantitative approaches to investing—building quantitative models to predict risk, return, and cost—and optimizing investment portfolios on the basis of those forecasts. Quantitative investing is a specific form of systematic investing. I do not argue here that all investing should become quantitative investing, but I do argue that investing is becoming increasingly systematic.

Acknowledgements

Many thanks to BlackRock and its senior leaders, Larry Fink and Rob Kapito, for supporting this effort and for deftly steering the firm toward the future. Many thanks also to Raffaele Savi and Jeff Shen, co-heads of the Systematic Active Equity team, and to Mark Wiseman, head of active equities, for their support and forward thinking.

Richard Grinold provided most of my early education in finance and investing and has heavily influenced my thinking on the future of investment management, as well as most other topics in investing. He has been a fantastic mentor, colleague, and co-author. His hand is quite visible in this book, most obviously in Chapter 4, on insights into active management. The mistakes and misunderstandings, though, belong solely to me.

Over the course of this work, I've benefited from the insight, advice, and help of many other people. Within the Systematic Active Equity team, Jeff and Raffaele provided the initial suggestion for a talk on this topic and, through many discussions, influenced my thinking about it. Brad Betts provided the vision for how big data and machine learning could affect investing and taught me much of what I know about those fields. Mike Lemmon co-authored several articles with me on smart beta/factor investing that provide key elements of the narrative. Mike Bishopp added early thoughts on active return decompositions and later thoughts on fees. Gerry Garvey provided insights into the intellectual developments of the field. Debbie McCoy suggested many improvements to the section on investing beyond returns. And Nikita Artizov and Sheng Xie helped with some detailed data analysis.

Beyond the Systematic Active Equity team, Mark Paltrowitz provided useful insights into various reasons why active management could succeed. Ed Fishwick shared his thoughts on many topics, including the drivers of success in fundamental active management. Ed's numerous invitations to present at the annual London Quant Group seminar provided opportunities to test out some of these ideas. Hubert De Jesus helped with his clear analysis of the changing trading environment. I benefited from a number of suggestions from BlackRock participants at presentations of this material. Although I have received help and suggestions from many people at BlackRock, this book represents my own views and not necessarily those of BlackRock.

Outside of BlackRock, Marty Leibowitz provided some early input to my thoughts on the future of investment management. Frank Jones, as usual, provided encouraging comments and suggestions. Matt Lyberg, the discussant for my presentation at the *Journal of Investment Management* conference in March 2017, provided useful feedback. Harry Marmer suggested many ideas during a lunch at the Q-Group. Will Goetzmann, whose book *Money Changes Everything* was a key source for the early history of investment management, and Larry Siegel both pointed me to papers by Geert Rouwenhorst on the Dutch investment trusts of the late 1700s.

I want to thank several people at Stellenbosch University: my host, Professor Christo Boshoff, for his gracious hospitality during my stay; Professor Stan du Plessis, dean of the Faculty of Economic and Management Sciences, for his support; and Dr. Mike Lamont, for suggesting me as a Thys Visser lecturer. I greatly benefited from the opportunity and from participant feedback. I also have many fond memories of the series of dinners Christo and Stan organized with different groups of academic and business leaders in Stellenbosch.

Larry Siegel encouraged me early on to write this book and then provided deft and insightful editing as I finished it. Thanks!

Finally, I want to thank my wife, Julia, for her enthusiastic proofreading and overall support in life.

1. Introduction

Investment management is in flux, arguably more than it has been in a long time. Active management is under pressure, with investors switching from active to index funds. New "smart beta" products offer low-cost exposures to many active ideas. Exchange-traded funds are proliferating. Markets and regulations have changed significantly over the past 10–20 years, and data and technology—which are increasingly important for investment management—are evolving even more rapidly.

In the midst of this change, what can we say about the future of investment management? What ideas will influence its evolution? What types of products will flourish over the next 5–10 years?

I use a long perspective to address these questions by exploring how investment management has grown and evolved to reach its current state, including key ideas and trends that have influenced its history. I analyze the modern intellectual history of investment management—roughly, the set of ideas, developed over the past 100 years, that have influenced investment management up to now. For additional context and to understand the full arc of history, I briefly discuss the early roots of the field. As I discuss this history, I review the various ideas and insights that ultimately coalesce into a coherent understanding of investing, in spite of its uncertain nature.

Over time, our understanding of risk has evolved from a general aversion to losing money to a precisely defined statistic we can measure and forecast. Our understanding of expected returns has evolved as the necessary data have become more available, as our understanding of fundamental value has developed, and as we have slowly come to understand the connection between return and risk and the relevance of human behavior to both. Data and technology have advanced in parallel to facilitate implementing better approaches.

Our systems of understanding this intrinsically uncertain activity of investing continue to expand, influencing the investment products we see today and those we expect to see in the future. It is as hard to imagine index funds and exchange-traded funds (ETFs) dominating the investment markets of the Netherlands in the 1700s as it is to imagine their absence in the global investment markets of 2018.

With an understanding of the ideas underlying investment management today, including several insights into active management, I discuss the many trends currently roiling the field. These trends, applied to the current state of investment management, suggest a specific view of the future.

The following is a roadmap for the rest of the book. Chapter 2, on the early roots of investment management, briefly explains what investment management is, what its required elements are, and when those elements first appeared. Investment management may go back to ancient times, but its clear historical record begins in the Netherlands in the late 1700s. Those early records show that investors already appreciated diversification and thought about value investing.

Chapter 3, on the modern history of investment management, traces the evolution of ideas and practices that have influenced the field up through today. The first efforts at developing systematic approaches began almost a century ago, partly in response to periods of wild speculation and losses, such as the market crash of 1929. Our understanding of investment value developed around this time, and our modern understanding of risk and portfolio construction began in the 1950s. Chapter 3 also traces the development of ideas underlying index funds—initially conceived in academia in the 1960s—and, in response, the eventual development of systematic approaches to active management.

Chapter 4, on seven insights into active management, describes key concepts required to understand efforts to outperform. This chapter begins with the "arithmetic of active management," the idea that active management is worse than a zero-sum game—that the average active manager will underperform. It then shows that the information ratio—the amount of outperformance per unit of risk—determines an active manager's ability to add value for investors. It also determines how investors should allocate risk and capital to different active products. The chapter discusses the fundamental law of active management, which breaks down the information ratio into constituent parts: skill, diversification, and efficiency. This relationship can help active managers develop new strategies and provide some guidance to investors looking to choose active managers. Other insights cover the process of forecasting returns, challenges to testing new investment ideas, and understanding how portfolio constraints affect the efficiency of implementing investment ideas.

Chapter 5, on seven trends in investment management, turns the spotlight on current directions that will affect the future of the field. These trajectories include the shift in assets from active to passive investing, the increase in competition among active managers, the changing market environment, the emergence of big data, the development of smart beta, the increased interest in what I call *investing beyond returns*—that is, investing for non-return objectives, such as environmental, social, and governance goals, as well as to earn returns—and, finally, fee compression.

Chapter 6, on the future of investment management, applies these trends to the current state of investment management—theory and practice—to forecast how the field will evolve over the next 5–10 years.

To add an optimistic spin on the current level of disruption in investment management, which is unsettling for many people in the field, I argue that this disruption can create great opportunities. The shifting boundaries between active and passive and dramatic changes in technology augur well for new types of products and new sources of information to help managers outperform. Today may not be a great time to be a 50-year-old investment manager, but as I often tell students and colleagues studying for the CFA® Program exams, it is a great time to be a quantitatively oriented 28-year-old entering the field.

2. The Early Roots of Investment Management

History is just one damn thing after another.

—*Arnold J. Toynbee*[1]

Analyzing the future of investment management requires context. How can we tell where we're going if we don't know where we've been? I argue that the history of investment management follows a long arc, and it bends toward increasingly systematic approaches.

This is not ultimately a history book, however, and I mainly focus on investment management from the perspective of the 21st century, where specially trained and often chartered professionals manage other people's money. These professionals invest funds across publicly traded stocks, bonds, managed funds, real estate, alternatives, and other opportunities on the basis of readily available information. And they manage investments for specific purposes—risk control (e.g., diversification), income, or growth; or funding retirement, education, or a home purchase. An individual owning his own business may be engaged in a worthwhile endeavor, but it isn't investment management by this definition. The profession began only when it became possible to at least somewhat easily invest in multiple opportunities.

Before I delve into the modern history of investment management, however, it's interesting to briefly see how far back we can trace the profession, including its key components: a broad range of available investments and the data to inform investment decisions. That is the focus of this chapter on the early roots of investment management.

Pre-Modern History: The Early Roots of Investment Management

According to William Goetzmann (2016), a variety of investment opportunities existed as far back as roughly 4,000 years ago. Ancient Mesopotamia had a functioning secondary loan market in personal promissory notes as well as opportunities for equity-like investments in maritime expeditions.[2] Thus, we know that early investors could have diversified. However, we don't know the availability of useful information about these investments back then, and

---

[1]Toynbee (1957, p. 267).

[2]These included limited liability and broad participation. Even ordinary (non-wealthy) citizens invested, according to Goetzmann.

we don't know whether professionals managed such investments for other people back then. Later, Athenian bankers may have acted as intermediaries in investing for clients, but if they did, we don't know much about the principles involved.

There is evidence from Rome in the first two centuries BCE that Roman publican societies (*societas publicanorum*) "anticipated the modern corporation and, in particular, the use of fungible shares with limited liability."[3] In the centuries when Rome was expanding but before it had its own extensive bureaucracy, these publican societies were government contractors and handled many government tasks, from building to tax collection. Shares in these societies were liquid and traded—with time-varying share prices—near the Temple of Castor in the Roman Forum. These societies effectively existed as separate entities, legally distinct from just a collection of owners. Thus, equity-like investment opportunities existed during part of the Roman era.

As for the component parts of investment management, government bonds appeared in Italy in the 12th century and full-scale bond markets developed a century later.

Financial historians have long studied when public companies first appeared. Public companies feature large numbers of minority owners who can freely buy and sell stakes without affecting the company. The company acts as an independent entity, represented by managers rather than a collection of owners, and it is the entity that becomes the bearer of obligations. These characteristics describe what are known as joint stock companies. The other important characteristic of public companies is limited liability. As we have seen, the publican societies in Rome had the characteristics of public companies, though they disappeared during the last centuries of the Roman era. Public companies reappeared in a few instances in Europe as early as the late 1300s.[4] And with the establishment of the Dutch East India Company in 1602—a joint stock limited liability company established by the Dutch government—public companies were here to stay and play a significant role in the world economy. Shares of the Dutch East India Company began trading on the Amsterdam Stock Exchange, which is generally viewed as the

---

[3]Malmendier (2005, p. 32).

[4]Goetzmann (2016), elaborating on Ibbotson and Brinson (1993), reported that the first publicly traded equity in medieval Europe was that of the Bazacle water mill near Toulouse, France. The shares traded continuously from 1372 until the company was nationalized by Électricité de France in 1946. Ibbotson and Brinson (1993, p. 149) noted that the mill itself dated to the 800s, but "by the 1100s ownership had been divided into shares, which were sometimes traded." Goetzmann (2016) reported that in 1372, it reorganized as a public company.

first stock market—though, as we have seen, something like a stock market existed in the Roman Forum. The Dutch East India Company offered shares broadly to anyone who could afford them, and they traded actively on this secondary market.

Interestingly, the so-called Glorious Revolution in England in 1688 brought the concept of joint stock limited liability companies from the Netherlands to England, where it flourished. In the Glorious Revolution, the Dutchman William III, Prince of Orange, in concert with English members of Parliament, invaded England, deposed the Catholic King James II, and became King of England. His wife, Mary, daughter of James II, became Queen of England.

According to Goetzmann (2016), in 1695, joint stock companies represented 1.3% of British national wealth, but that amount rose to 13% by 1720 during the South Sea Bubble.

The South Sea Company, founded in 1711, was a British joint stock company originated for two somewhat orthogonal purposes. First, as the name implied, it had the British monopoly on trade with South America, which was potentially quite lucrative. Second, it represented a feat of financial engineering designed to address Britain's huge national debt. Owners of illiquid British debt could swap those holdings for shares in the South Sea Company, which paid a dividend yield less than the debt coupon, but the shares were liquid and provided a stake in the South American trade. Meanwhile, the British government consolidated much of its debt into a loan from the South Sea Corporation at a lower interest rate. The government officials who developed this plan became directors and significant shareholders of the company.

Although many people interested in investing or European history have heard of the South Sea Company and its stock bubble, few people are aware that a significant part of the South American trade consisted of Britain supplying African slaves to the Spanish colonies in South America. The South Sea Company owned the contractual right (*asiento*) that Spain provided to Britain for that slave trade.

In 1719, the South Sea Company was engaged in another exchange of shares for British debt, which would be more favorable for the company at higher share prices (they would, therefore, exchange fewer shares for the debt). The company spread false rumors of the value of South American trade, leading to an enormous run-up in its price. This scheme came crashing down in 1720, leading to widespread ruin among shareholders, many of whom purchased shares on margin. As this turmoil played out, Parliament passed the Bubble Act of 1720, greatly restricting the creation and trading of joint stock companies. It required, among other things, a royal charter or act of Parliament to create a joint stock company. This situation didn't change until the mid-1800s.[5]

Another component of investment management is the availability and use of information required to make thoughtful investments. Stock price lists appeared in 1691, in John Houghton's *Collection for Improvement of Husbandry and Trade*,[6] and by 1694 the publication regularly listed 52 traded companies. For the largest of them, Houghton provided free weekly price quotes. Subscribers had to pay for price quotes for the smaller firms.

Overall, we can trace components of investment management back quite far, and somewhat recognizable investment management may also have existed during certain periods in that era. But the most concrete and clear evidence of early investment management occurred in the Netherlands starting in 1774, more than 240 years ago.

The Dutch Origins of Investment Management

The first broadly available investment trust—where investors could purchase shares in a diversified portfolio of investments—appeared in the Netherlands in 1774.[7] It was effectively the world's first mutual fund.

In July 1774, Abraham van Ketwich invited investors to consider Eendragt Maakt Magt, the first closed-end investment trust. The name means "unity creates strength." It's both a motto of the Dutch Republic and a succinct argument for diversification. Evidently, the history of providing investment opportunities with clever names goes back to at least that time. The investment management goal of Eendragt Maakt Magt was solely diversification. The trust invested in a portfolio of foreign government bonds from Austria, Denmark, Germany, Spain, Sweden, and Russia as well as plantation mortgages from the West Indies. This investment vehicle would appeal to smaller investors who lacked the ability to diversify across so many different bonds. The bonds in the portfolio had face values of 1,000 guilders each, yet investors could buy shares in Eendragt Maakt Magt for only 500 guilders.

The fund prospectus specified details regarding initial portfolio formation, including the goal of equal proportions of investments across many different issues in each of several categories. These details significantly limited any flexibility to adjust the portfolio weights or holdings, adding to the

---

[5]Because of the Bubble Act, much of the industrial revolution (roughly 1760 to 1820–1840) was financed not by joint stock companies but by partnerships of wealthy individuals without limited liability.

[6]Goetzmann (2016, p. 327).

[7]Rouwenhorst (2016).

evidence that Eendragt Maakt Magt's raison d'être was diversification, not active management.

The risk control extended beyond diversification. The prospectus also specified that van Ketwich would store the physical securities in his office, in an iron chest with three differently working locks to which the trust commissioners and the notary public kept the separate keys.[8]

Eendragt Maakt Magt promised to pay an annual dividend of 4%, with adjustments over time based on the actual income produced. The plan was to dissolve the trust after 25 years and distribute any remaining proceeds to investors. Oddly, given its goal of diversification and risk mitigation, Eendragt Maakt Magt also included a lottery component that used some of the investment proceeds to—by lot—retire some shares at a premium and increase dividends to some shares. According to Rouwenhorst, this lottery-like feature, which included the small probability of a significantly higher return, appeared to be designed to attract small investors.

Why did the first mutual fund appear in the Netherlands in 1774? Circumstantial evidence points to a motivation for financial innovation that plays out many times after this: a response to a financial crisis. In this case, it was the credit crisis of 1772. Credit had expanded in the years before then, leading to increased speculation. But in mid-1772, a partner at a British bank fled to France to avoid repaying debts, initiating a credit collapse. Many British firms went bankrupt, and Dutch banks suffered significant losses as well. Van Ketwich would have experienced this crisis up close and seen the need for lower-risk investment opportunities.

Interestingly, the British East India Company struggled to repay debts to the Bank of England during this period, leading it to try to raise money by selling its vast inventory of tea to the 13 British colonies in America. Parliament passed the Tea Act to facilitate this effort, giving the British East India Company a monopoly over the tea trade in the Colonies. This situation led to protests, including the Boston Tea Party in 1773.

After the launch of Eendragt Maakt Magt, more than 30 other funds started up in the Netherlands at the end of the 1700s. One interesting example is Concordia Res Parvae Crescunt,[9] the second fund launched by van Ketwich and the third fund overall. Designed to provide diversification, this fund also allowed flexibility in managing the portfolio. According to Rouwenhorst, the prospectus declared that the fund would invest in "solid securities and those

---

[8]Rouwenhorst (2016, p. 223).
[9]The name comes from the Latin origin of Eendragt Maakt Magt, according to Rouwenhorst (2016, p. 217).

that, based on a decline in their price, … could be purchased below their intrinsic values," making this possibly the world's first value fund.[10]

Eendragt Maakt Magt redeemed its last shares in 1824, 50 years after it started. Concordia Res Parvae Crescunt redeemed its last shares in 1894, a full 114 years after launch. Both funds started with a plan to dissolve after a period of time, yet Concordia Res Parvae Crescunt ended up becoming one of the longest-lived funds of all time.

The Evolution of Investment Management in Britain and the United States

Following the Dutch origins of investment management, a somewhat parallel set of developments occurred in Britain and the United States during the 1800s.

First was a set of advances that revitalized public investing in company stocks. As we have seen, there was great enthusiasm for equity investing in England in the early 1700s, up until the South Sea Bubble. At that time in England, significant numbers of joint stock companies with limited liability existed. Broad public acceptance of equity investing required the existence of many joint stock companies with limited liability, and the Bubble Act of 1720 essentially eliminated them.

Revitalization of equity investing began with the Joint Stock Companies Act of 1844, 124 years after the Bubble Act, which established procedures for anyone to start a joint stock company (i.e., to incorporate). Prior to this act of Parliament, the Bubble Act allowed the creation of a joint stock company only by either royal charter or an act of legislation. Hence, many businesses operated as unincorporated associations with potentially large numbers of associated members. This situation could be quite unwieldy. For instance, any litigation needed to be done in the name of all the members, requiring all of their sign-offs.

The Limited Liability Act of 1855 then allowed limited liability for joint stock companies established by the general public (i.e., under the Joint Stock Companies Act of 1844). So, by 1855, companies could easily incorporate and set up limited liability structures. This made equity investment management possible, by allowing the creation of large numbers of joint stock, limited liability companies.

In 1868, the Foreign and Colonial Government Trust became the first British mutual fund. According to its prospectus, its goal was to provide "the investor of moderate means the same advantages as the large capitalist

---

[10]Rouwenhorst (2016, p. 217).

9

in diminishing the risk of investing ... by spreading the investment over a number of different stocks" (*stocks* meaning what we would call *bonds*).[11] It changed its name to the Foreign and Colonial Investment Trust in 1891 and first invested in equities in 1925. It still exists today—the world's oldest investment trust. It is a closed-end fund trading on both the London Stock Exchange and the New Zealand Stock Exchange.

After the launch of this first British investment trust, several additional trusts were launched in England over the subsequent decade. Investment trusts began in the United States in the 1890s. The first US open-end mutual fund, the Massachusetts Investors Trust, began in 1924. It survived an 83% drop during the 1929–32 crash and still exists today.

The Evolution of Investment Data

As previously noted, stock price lists appeared in 1691, in John Houghton's oddly named *Collection for Improvement of Husbandry and Trade*. John Castaing's *Course of the Exchange* began publishing daily stock prices in 1693 and was the main source of stock price data into the 1800s.

The listings of stock prices dropped off dramatically, along with the trading of stocks, after the South Sea Bubble of 1720. But by the 1800s, a number of data providers covered the rapidly growing number of potential investments. The *Economist* magazine appeared in 1843. It offered a monthly list of stock and bond prices that was more than 50 pages long.

Paul Reuter started Reuters in 1851, relying on the telegraph and more than 200 carrier pigeons to transmit information quickly. Henry Poor started Poor's Publishing, an investment information service, in 1860. In 1941, it combined with Standard Statistics Bureau (founded in 1906) to form Standard & Poor's. Dow Jones began in 1882, and the *Financial Times* started up in 1888.

These companies mainly provided price data in those early days. Available fundamental information about companies was limited, inconsistent, and poorly regulated. In the United States prior to the 1930s, individual states handled regulations, leading to inconsistencies across the country. The situation improved in England in 1908 with passage of the Companies (Consolidation) Act, which required disclosures in annual reports. But in the United States, many companies kept sales figures secret, even into the 1920s.

Interestingly, in 1909, Henry Lowenfeld wrote *Investment: An Exact Science*, wherein he proposed his theory of the "Geographic Distribution of Capital"—the idea that an investment portfolio should be diversified across

---

[11]Bullock (1959, p. 2).

different economic zones around the world. This wasn't exactly a new idea; it was the concept underlying Eendragt Maagt Makt in 1774. But Lowenfeld correctly understood that different economic zones faced different risks and that diversification could reduce risk without affecting expected return ("income" in his analysis). And economic zone of origin as well as industry were fundamental variables widely available even in the absence of other fundamental data. The definition and analysis of diversification would become much more precise less than 50 years later.

Bibliography

Bullock, Hugh. 1959. *The Story of Investment Companies*. New York: Columbia University Press.

Goetzmann, William N. 2016. *Money Changes Everything: How Finance Made Civilization Possible*. Princeton, NJ: Princeton University Press.

Ibbotson, Roger G., and Gary P. Brinson. 1993. *Global Investing: The Professional's Guide to the World Capital Markets*. New York: McGraw-Hill.

Lowenfeld, Henry. 1909. *Investment: An Exact Science*. London: Financial Review of Reviews.

Malmendier, Ulrike. 2005. "Roman Shares." In *The Origins of Value: The Financial Innovations That Created Modern Capital Markets*, edited by W. Goetzmann and G. Rouwenhorst. Oxford, UK: Oxford University Press.

Rouwenhorst, Geert K. 2016. "Structural Finance and the Origins of Mutual Funds in 18th Century Netherlands." In *Financial Market History: Reflections on the Past for Investors Today*, edited by David Chambers and Elroy Dimson. Charlottesville, VA: CFA Institute Research Foundation.

Rubinstein, Mark. 2006. *A History of the Theory of Investments*. Hoboken, NJ: John Wiley & Sons, Inc.

Toynbee, Arnold J. 1957. "Law and Freedom in History." In *A Study of History*, Vol. 2. Oxford, UK: Oxford University Press.

3. The Modern History of Investment Management

History is written by the survivors.

—Modern proverb

Chapter 2 traced the roots of investment management back to the earliest availability of multiple investment opportunities and the origins of investment data. It focused more on where activities began than on the ideas that informed how people invested. In many cases, we don't know how they invested, though the understanding of the value of diversification goes back quite far. In this chapter, on the modern history of investment management, the ideas informing investors play a central role. Peter Bernstein (1992) covered some of this terrain in his book *Capital Ideas*. Bernstein conveyed these ideas without mathematics, but I've included equations where I think they add clarity. By the early 1900s, many of the required elements of investment management existed at some level, including a wide variety of available liquid bond and stock investments and some information to help inform investors. Henry Lowenfeld (1909) had even proposed his "exact science" approach to investing by diversifying across geographic regions. But it took the stock market crash of 1929 to inspire a last set of developments that characterize what I call the beginning of the modern era.

The Origins of Systematic Investing

In response to the stock market crash, new rules and regulations required the disclosure of financial statements and the independent audit of those statements by public accountants. In the United States, these new regulations were contained in the Securities Act of 1933 and the Securities Exchange Act of 1934. The first governed new issues, and the second governed secondary trading of issues. Following these changes, investors gained access to reliable, material information about possible investments. This access finally facilitated the first modern systematic approaches to investing.

Benjamin Graham, David Dodd, and *Security Analysis*. If the first step on the path to systematic investing was a rudimentary understanding of diversification, then the second step may have been the publication of Graham and Dodd's *Security Analysis* in 1934.[12] Though the book discussed

---

[12]Graham and Dodd (2009).

bonds as well as stocks, Mark Rubinstein (2006, p. 66) called this "perhaps the most famous book written on the stock market," and it has long been the Bible of security analysis and value investing.

Written against the backdrop of the wild speculation that characterized the run-up to the crash of 1929, *Security Analysis* made several important contributions that remain valid. First, it argued for the critical importance of thorough and rigorous analysis—hard work—before making any investment decision. Although this idea seems obvious, it was not common prior to Graham and Dodd's work; in fact, there wasn't much of a framework for analyzing securities. Graham and Dodd provided the necessary framework by presenting a systematic approach to analyzing securities—especially dividends, earnings, and the balance sheet. Peter Bernstein told a story about Ben Graham analyzing Consolidated Edison, a hot stock in 1928: "Most people believed, on the basis of the truncated and incomplete reporting permitted by regulators in those days, that the dividends being paid by the company represented only a small portion of the actual earnings of its operating subsidiaries."[13] Graham actually went to City Hall, researched the utility company records there, and discovered that Con Ed's subsidiaries generated negligible earnings. "When Graham published his findings, one of the stockbrokers he was working with took him aside and said, 'Young man, it is people like you who are going to destroy this business.'"[14] *Security Analysis* encouraged investors to "take very much the same attitude in valuing shares of stock as in valuing his own business,"[15] a view often repeated by Ben Graham's most famous and successful disciple, Warren Buffett. Graham and Dodd also noted that in the 30 or so years before publication of their book, there "was a considerable advance in the frequency and adequacy of corporate statements, thus supplying the public and the securities analyst with a wealth of statistical data."[16]

The book distinguished investing from speculation. According to Graham and Dodd, "an investment operation is one which, upon thorough analysis, promises safety of principal and a satisfactory return. Operations not meeting these requirements are speculative."[17] Basically, Graham and Dodd tried to distinguish their approach to investing from the gambling—buying stocks on rumor and because they were going up—that characterized the run-up to October 1929. Finally, the book introduced the concept of a *margin of*

---

[13]Bernstein (1992, p. 157).
[14]Ibid.
[15]Graham and Dodd (2009, p. 409)
[16]Graham and Dodd (2009, p. 349).
[17]Graham and Dodd (2009, p. 106).

　　　　13

safety. As Bruce Greenwald noted, "The purchase of securities should then be made only at prices far enough below the intrinsic value to provide a margin of safety that would offer appropriate protection against this 'indistinctness' in the calculated intrinsic value."[18] Here was the Graham and Dodd focus on value. They understood that we cannot estimate intrinsic value precisely, and so they advocated investing in securities whose prices are so low relative to intrinsic value that margins of safety exist to counteract that uncertainty. Much of *Security Analysis* described systematically how to analyze various types of securities: bonds, preferred stock, convertibles, and common stock. The book then focused in on understanding and then predicting earnings and the balance sheet.

Although Graham and Dodd's book represented a breakthrough in investment management—and it is still widely read today—it provided a very useful set of rules rather than a theory of investing. It doesn't fully consider diversification or the role of risk in investment value. Ben Graham later commented that investors should own "a minimum of ten different issues and a maximum of about thirty."[19] Finally, *Security Analysis* generally avoids any sophisticated mathematical analysis. That soon arrived, however, in 1938 with John Burr Williams's *The Theory of Investment Value.*

John Burr Williams and *The Theory of Investment Value.* *The Theory of Investment Value*, which, like *Security Analysis*, appeared against the backdrop of the crash of 1929 and the subsequent Great Depression, is a remarkable book from today's perspective. It truly is a theory of investment value, and it is one we still use today. John Burr Williams is widely acknowledged for identifying investment value as the discounted value of future dividends. The value of a company must be its future payments to investors, discounted back to today. With that framework, the book analyzes in detail many possible paths of future dividends.

With that core principle, John Burr Williams (1938) provided at least two other gems of analysis. His "Law of the Conservation of Investment Value" showed that value is independent of the capital structure of the firm (i.e., how the firm is financed between equity and bond offerings). Modigliani and Miller formalized this idea in 1958, and it partly contributed to their winning Nobel Prizes. (They provided a more rigorous proof of this idea, but it also seems that *The Theory of Investment Value* was not widely known or appreciated back then.) Williams also developed algebraic formulas for investment value in many particular cases, including constant dividend growth, almost

---

[18]Bruce Greenwald in Graham and Dodd (2009, p. 536).
[19]Graham (1973, p. 114).

two decades ahead of Gordon's 1956 model. The book provided several key observations, whether or not recognized. Beyond these specific contributions, John Burr Williams also advanced the use of sophisticated mathematics in understanding investments. As he noted in the preface to the book, "The mathematics is not to be considered as a drawback to the analysis. Quite the contrary! The truth is that the mathematical method is a new tool of great power, whose use promises to lead to notable advances in investment analysis."[20] That has certainly proven true. Williams's path to publication was rather interesting as it turns out. The book was his PhD dissertation in economics at Harvard University, and he submitted it for publication prior to receiving his degree, which caused some difficulty for him within the department. Some publishers refused to consider the book because of its extensive mathematics, and Harvard University Press published it only after Williams agreed to cover part of the printing cost.

We can trace the origins of systematic investing mainly back to the United States in the 1930s. After the stock market crash, we saw new regulations requiring financial disclosures and the publication of *Security Analysis* and *The Theory of Investment Value*. These events set the stage for modern portfolio theory.

The Birth of Modern Portfolio Theory

Modern portfolio theory began with Harry Markowitz mathematically defining risk. This section on the birth of modern portfolio theory begins with him and follows through to the launch of the first index fund.

Harry Markowitz and *Portfolio Selection*. According to Harry Markowitz (1990), "the basic concepts of portfolio theory came to me one afternoon in the library while reading John Burr Williams' *Theory of Investment Value*." First published in 1952, Markowitz's "Portfolio Selection" mathematically defined risk as the standard deviation of return and proposed that portfolio selection should follow from the optimal trade-off between expected return and risk. Before Markowitz, investors understood risk as roughly related to the probability of loss. By providing a precise mathematical definition of risk—and one that accorded well with investor intuition—Markowitz dramatically opened investment management to mathematical analysis. Furthermore, by defining investment management as the trade-off between *portfolio* expected return and risk, he placed the portfolio center stage. The standard deviation of a portfolio return depends on the standard

---

[20]Williams (1938, p. ix).

deviations of the returns to all the assets in the portfolio, as well as the correlations of returns to all those assets. Markowitz proposed that all investors should care about in the end is the behavior of the portfolio, not the individual assets in it. Let's look at this in a bit more mathematical detail.[21] If a portfolio P invests a fraction $h_P(n)$ in asset n, σ_n represents the standard deviation of asset n's return (which we also call asset n's volatility), and ρ_{nm} is the correlation between the returns to assets n and m, then

$$\sigma_P^2 = \sum_{n=1}^{N} h_P^2(n) \cdot \sigma_n^2 + \sum_{n \neq m} h_P(n) \cdot h_P(m) \cdot \sigma_n \cdot \sigma_m \cdot \rho_{nm}. \tag{3.1}$$

That is, the variance of the portfolio's return, σ_P^2, equals the weighted sum of the variances of the individual asset returns plus a weighted sum of the covariances of each asset with every other asset. (Variance is the square of standard deviation, σ.)

We can also write this more simply in vector notation as

$$\sigma_P^2 = \mathbf{h}_P^T \cdot \mathbf{V} \cdot \mathbf{h}_P. \tag{3.2}$$

Equations 3.1 and 3.2 say exactly the same thing. Equation 3.2 is more compact,[22] representing the portfolio as

$$\mathbf{h}_P = \begin{bmatrix} h_P(1) \\ h_P(2) \\ \vdots \\ h_P(N) \end{bmatrix} \tag{3.3}$$

and the covariance matrix, $\mathbf{V}$, as

$$\mathbf{V} = \begin{pmatrix} \sigma_1^2 & \cdots & \sigma_{1N} \\ \vdots & \ddots & \vdots \\ \sigma_{N1} & \cdots & \sigma_N^2 \end{pmatrix}, \tag{3.4}$$

---

[21]For simplicity, I use the notation from Grinold and Kahn (2000).

[22]We represent vectors and matrices in bold (non-italicized) type and scalar numbers in standard (not bold) type. (Vectors are matrices with one dimension equal to 1.) You can see this, for example, in Equation 3.2. On the right-hand side of the equal sign, we multiply together a vector times a matrix times a vector. The result is a scalar number—the portfolio variance.

where

$$\sigma_{ij} = \sigma_i \cdot \sigma_j \cdot \rho_{ij}. \tag{3.5}$$

Thus, Equations 3.1 and 3.2 tell us that the risk, or standard deviation, of the portfolio is lower than the weighted sum of the standard deviations of the portfolio components, where the correlation matrix of the component returns determines the amount by which it's lower. All other things being equal, lower correlations mean lower overall portfolio risk.

If all the assets are uncorrelated and have the same volatility and we invest equal amounts in every asset, then

$$h_p(n) = \frac{1}{N}$$

$$\sigma_n = \sigma \text{ (each asset } n \text{ has identical standard deviation)} \tag{3.6}$$

$$\sigma_p \Rightarrow \frac{\sigma}{\sqrt{N}}.$$

For example, if we equally invest in 20 uncorrelated assets, each with a volatility of 35%, our portfolio will have a volatility of about 8%.

With the same assumptions above except that the correlations aren't zero but, rather, every asset has the same correlation ρ with every other asset, then in the limit of a large number of assets N in the portfolio,

$$\sigma_p \Rightarrow \sigma \cdot \sqrt{\rho}. \tag{3.7}$$

Using the same example as before but now assuming the assets are all 50% correlated with each other (i.e., $\rho = 0.5$), the portfolio volatility is about 25%, much higher than when we assumed no correlations.

In general, assets vary in the standard deviations of their returns, the correlations between assets can vary, and investors do not invest equal fractions in every asset. Equation 3.1 (or, equivalently, Equation 3.2) provides the general result.

The importance of asset correlations deserves special attention here. One reason that Graham and Dodd, as well as Williams, may have ignored risk is the idea that investors can reduce risk without limit by diversifying across a number of assets. That's basically the result in Equation 3.6. The more assets, the lower the risk. But the Markowitz framework and our example show that that isn't quite right. Asset correlations limit the extent to which diversification can reduce risk. If every asset is correlated with every other asset, we are

17

Exhibit 3.1. The Markowitz Efficient Frontier

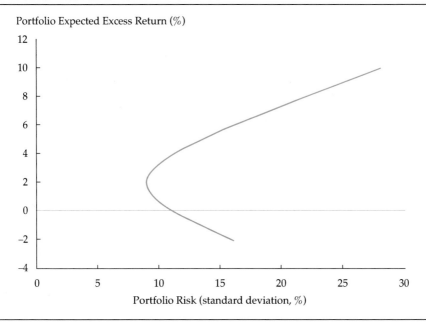

Portfolio Expected Excess Return (%)

Portfolio Risk (standard deviation, %)

closer to the situation captured by Equation 3.7. We later see that detailed factor models of risk can provide useful insights into the structure of investment markets.

After defining risk, Markowitz (1952) proposed that investors care about both expected return and risk. We can take every possible feasible fully invested portfolio,[23] calculate its expected return and risk, and represent it as a point on a graph of expected return against risk. He showed that there is a set of *efficient* portfolios on that graph. They are the portfolios with the lowest risk for every level of expected return (or equivalently the portfolios with the highest expected return for all portfolios with the same risk). **Exhibit 3.1** illustrates this concept. The curve traces the minimum standard deviation portfolio for each expected return.

Investors should choose from among those efficient portfolios. Different investors might choose different efficient portfolios on the basis of their own risk preferences. An investor with a higher tolerance for risk will choose a higher-risk (and higher-expected-return) portfolio.

This says something remarkable. If we can forecast returns and risks, investment management is then a mathematical optimization problem.

---

[23]We represent a portfolio as a set of holdings (e.g., 10% in A, 5% in B, 0% in C, and so on).

Mathematical optimization identifies the efficient frontier. Then, on the basis of risk tolerance, investors can choose the best portfolio for themselves among those efficient portfolios. For the first time, we have a clearly specified framework for portfolio management. As Peter Bernstein (2007, p. xii) noted, "Before Markowitz's 1952 essay on portfolio selection, there was no genuine theory of portfolio construction—there were just rules of thumb and folklore."

It is important to remember that Markowitz proposed this idea at the beginning of the computer age. At the time, it was basically a purely academic idea. In 1952, the only computers capable of performing such an analysis existed at US government labs focused on nuclear weapon design. It would take further developments in both theory and computing for Markowitz to have a practical impact on investing. By the time he won the Nobel Prize in 1990, his approach had had a significant impact indeed.

Looking back at the early 1950s, we already have a rigorous, if somewhat abstract, risk–return framework. We have a systematic approach to security analysis, which could, in principle, lead to better estimates of expected returns and the construction of portfolios with higher expected returns per unit of risk taken. However, no investors were fully utilizing this approach to investment management. The necessary computing power wasn't readily available, and few investors had sufficient training in the required mathematics and econometrics. The next steps in this evolution of modern portfolio theory came from William F. Sharpe, a student of Harry Markowitz.

William Sharpe and the Capital Asset Pricing Model. Sharpe (1963) first developed a simplified risk model to facilitate Markowitz portfolio construction. There were at least two practical challenges to implementing the Markowitz approach. First, to estimate the standard deviation for a portfolio of N assets required estimates of not only N standard deviations (one for each asset) but also $\dfrac{N \cdot (N-1)}{2}$ correlations (for every asset with every other asset). So, for three assets A, B, and C, we need three correlations: the correlations of A with B, A with C, and B with C. As N increases, the number of required parameters grows quickly. Second, as N increases, the required computing time also grows rapidly.

Sharpe introduced a simplified model of asset returns, separating each return into two components. To be exact, Sharpe focused on excess returns (r_n), the returns above the risk-free return (e.g., the return to investing in a US Treasury bill). The excess return to asset n consists of a systematic piece (driven by r_{mkt}, the excess return to the market) and a residual piece, θ_n, independent of the market:

$$r_n = \beta_n \cdot r_{mkt} + \theta_n. \tag{3.8}$$

The *beta* coefficient, β_n, measures asset n's exposure to the market. If we, for example, plotted monthly excess returns to asset n versus monthly excess market returns over a five-year period, we could estimate β_n as the slope of the line that best fits those points.

Now we can always do this: Break every return into two such components, one correlated with the market and one independent of the market. But Sharpe made the *assumption* that all residual returns are uncorrelated. By construction, the residual returns for each asset are uncorrelated with the market. Sharpe's assumption was that they were also uncorrelated with each other. For different assets n and m,

$$\text{Corr}\{\theta_n, \theta_m\} = 0. \tag{3.9}$$

So, any two different assets are correlated because, and only because, both are exposed to the market. Mathematically,

$$\text{Corr}\{r_n, r_m\} = \frac{\beta_n \cdot \beta_m \cdot \sigma_{mkt}^2}{\sigma_n \cdot \sigma_m}. \tag{3.10}$$

Instead of estimating $\frac{N \cdot (N+1)}{2}$ risk parameters (standard deviations and correlations), we now need to estimate only $2N + 1$ parameters—the $\{\beta_n\}$, the $\{\sigma_n\}$, and σ_{mkt}. We have reduced the number of required parameters once we have four or more assets, and we have reduced the number of required parameters significantly once we have many more than four assets. For 500 assets, we need estimate only 1,001 parameters instead of 125,250 parameters. This simplified model also significantly reduces computing time.

In his 1963 article, Sharpe stated that solving a 100-asset problem on an IBM 7090 computer required 33 minutes, but his simplified risk model reduced that to 30 seconds. In what might be even more surprising to today's readers, he further stated that the IBM 7090 he was using could handle only 249 assets at most, whereas using the simplified risk model allowed him to handle 2,000 assets.

Sharpe's simplified risk model had significant benefits in reducing the required number of estimated parameters and computer speed. Unfortunately, it didn't predict risk especially well. The assumption that asset residual returns are uncorrelated breaks down too often. It says, for example, that ExxonMobil and Royal Dutch Shell, two large oil companies, are correlated only because both are exposed to the overall market, ignoring the many oil-related characteristics and large-stock characteristics they also share. I return later to risk models that provide greater structure, simplicity, and accuracy. But for now, let's look at Sharpe's next effort, seemingly inspired in part by his simplified model (though the two make different assumptions).

In 1964, Sharpe (and separately, Lintner 1965, Mossin 1966, and Treynor 1961) proposed an equilibrium model of expected returns and pricing: the capital asset pricing model, or CAPM. If investors share the same views of expected returns and risks (a rather heroic assumption) but differ in their aversion to risk, they will agree on the Markowitz efficient frontier, which depends only on expected return and risk.

Sharpe then showed, using the mathematics associated with optimization, that expected excess returns for any portfolio (or asset) are simply related to the expected excess return to Portfolio Q, the efficient portfolio with the highest ratio of expected return to risk. **Exhibit 3.2** shows Q graphically.

What Sharpe said mathematically is

$$E\{r_p\} = \beta_P \cdot E\{r_Q\}. \tag{3.11}$$

Exhibit 3.2.   Portfolio Q and the Markowitz Efficient Frontier

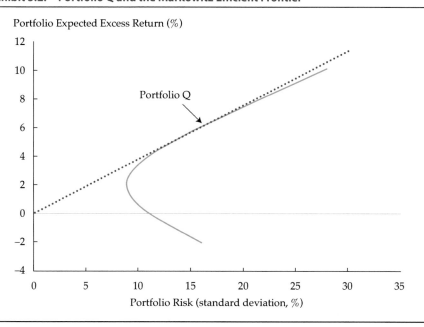

Portfolio Expected Excess Return (%)

Portfolio Q

Portfolio Risk (standard deviation, %)

It turns out that Equation 3.11 is always true, even if we aren't in equilibrium and investors do not agree on expected returns and risk. But in that case, every investor will have her own Portfolio Q. Sharpe's assumption that all investors agree on expected returns and risks means that they also all agree on Portfolio Q. Sharpe just needed a small step from there to assert that if all investors agree on Q and all are in equilibrium, then Q must be the market portfolio—that is, the capitalization-weighted combination of all the securities in the market. (If it weren't, then investors would trade away from the market toward Q, so they wouldn't be in equilibrium.) Therefore

$$E\{r_p\} = \beta_p \cdot E\{r_{mkt}\}. \tag{3.12}$$

These β coefficients are the same ones from the simplified risk model, though the two models make different assumptions. Sharpe's simplified risk model assumed residual returns are uncorrelated but didn't assume equilibrium or that all investors agree on expected returns and risks. The CAPM assumes equilibrium and that investors agree on expected returns and risks but does not assume that residual returns are uncorrelated. The β coefficients play roles in each model, though, and it is tempting to assume that Sharpe's simplified risk model somehow provided an inspiration on his journey to (co-) discover the CAPM.

The CAPM is the first theory of asset pricing with risk playing a central role. It also established the market as the benchmark for investors, laying the initial groundwork for index funds. If the market is efficient and has the highest ratio of expected return to risk, then investors should want to own it.

Of course, the CAPM relied on some heroic assumptions, and its definition of "the market" is actually the portfolio of everything: global stocks, bonds, real estate, commodities, collectibles, and so on—not something as narrow as, for example, the S&P 500 Index.

Still, this was a significant advance in our understanding of investing, and Sharpe shared the 1990 Nobel Prize in Economic Sciences with Harry Markowitz and Merton Miller.

Eugene Fama and the Efficient Market Hypothesis. If the CAPM first turned the market itself into an interesting portfolio for investors, Eugene Fama amplified the interest with his efficient market hypothesis (EMH), described in his review paper of 1970. By efficient market, he meant that prices reflect available information; thus, investors can only beat the market in expectation by taking more risk. (After the fact, their having taken more risk means that they might *not* beat the market; that is what "risk" means.)

Sharpe and others used equilibrium arguments to promote the market portfolio. Fama looked empirically at stock return distributions to argue that investors can beat the market only by taking more risk. He also argued that the activities of many different investors, each with their own views of expected returns, can lead to an efficient market.

In the details, Fama posited the by now well-known three forms of market efficiency: weak, semi-strong, and strong. In weak efficiency, market prices fully reflect historical price information. In semi-strong efficiency, they reflect all publicly available information. And in strong efficiency, prices reflect all relevant information, public and private.

These arguments, backed by Fama's empirical evidence and his sway over academic finance as a leading professor at the University of Chicago, added to the view of the market portfolio as the optimal portfolio. The efficient market hypothesis became the basic assumption active managers needed to overcome. And as sometimes happens in academia, the efficient market became such enforced dogma that it strongly discouraged any work on market inefficiency by finance and economics professors for the next 30 years or more, to the detriment of the ivory tower.

Victor Niederhoffer, in his 1997 autobiography *The Education of a Speculator*, illustrated this point with an anecdote from his time as a graduate student in the business school at the University of Chicago in the 1960s. He overhears four other grad students talking with two professors about research into how trading volume might influence stock prices. One of the grad students is concerned about the possibility of finding an effect that is inconsistent with the EMH. One of the professors reassures the student that they will deal with that in the unlikely event it occurs. As Niederhoffer (1997, p. 270) put it, "Here were six scientists openly hoping to find no departures from ignorance." Niederhoffer then says to them, "I sure am glad you are all keeping an open mind about your research."

This happened in spite of our inability to ever prove the efficient market hypothesis (in any of its forms). We can't prove such a hypothesis; we can only accumulate evidence in its favor. We might be able to use counterexamples to disprove a hypothesis, but even doing that is challenging in this case. We have seen the EMH fall short in the face of price bubbles or rapid price movements. When the S&P 500 fell by more than 20% on Monday, 19 October 1987, it was hard to argue that prices fully reflected available information on both Friday, 16 October 1987, and Monday, 19 October 1987. Could our entire information set have shifted by so much over a relatively uneventful weekend? It's highly unlikely. Yet, in spite of such counterexamples, the EMH seems to accurately capture the fact that beating the market is quite difficult. It has had a major impact on our understanding of markets, and Eugene Fama shared the Nobel Prize in Economic Sciences in 2013.

The First Index Fund. The final significant milestone in this "birth of modern portfolio theory" era occurred in 1971, when Wells Fargo Investment Advisors launched the first index fund, for the Samsonite Luggage Pension Plan.[24] Finally there was an actual investment product inspired by the academic work of Markowitz, Sharpe, Fama, and many others. Before Sharpe and Fama, in particular, the idea of just buying every stock in the market would have seemed a ludicrous proposition. Shouldn't careful security analysis inform investment decisions? Why settle for average? But starting in 1971, money started flowing into index funds, and those funds have kept growing ever since.

Given the enormous success of indexing—which we know with the perspective of 45+ years after that first launch—it's interesting to look at that first fund and its launch in more detail.

The first index fund was not designed to track the S&P 500. In fact, it invested in an *equal-weighted* portfolio of the roughly 1,500 stocks traded on the New York Stock Exchange. Managing this fund required a considerable technology infrastructure investment—who at that time managed portfolios with more than a thousand stocks? Furthermore, Wells Fargo quickly learned that an equal-weighted portfolio generates a lot of turnover. Every day (or every chosen rebalance period), the stocks move out of alignment and require rebalancing back to equal weights. This doesn't happen with capitalization-weighted indexes, such as the S&P 500. And in fact, the S&P 500 Index fund was "Version 2" for Samsonite.

As to the launch of the fund, Ancell (2012) and Jahnke (1990) provide a wonderful history of those early days. Here, it's worth asking two questions: Why Wells Fargo? Why Samsonite? Wells Fargo was not an investment management powerhouse at that time and was headquartered in San Francisco—not New York City or Boston, where many large investment management firms have headquarters. Wells Fargo wanted to grow its investment management business, but it had several challenges—its size and location, in particular. The firm knew it would have trouble besting the East Coast–based market leaders at their own game. When these modern portfolio theory ideas developed in academia, Wells Fargo saw them as a way to enter the field. It's not surprising, then, that a second-tier player in investment management launched the first index fund.

---

[24]The Vanguard 500 Index fund launched after the Samsonite fund. It was the first *retail* index fund.

As it turned out, Wells Fargo's bet on index funds and modern portfolio theory was ultimately quite successful. That initial fund—after many years, several corporate actions, and the launches of many more index funds globally—became a large part of BlackRock, the world's largest investment manager, with over $6 trillion in assets in 2018. But it was a bet that required remarkable patience. Wells Fargo didn't make money on index funds for the first 13 years.

The Samsonite Luggage pension fund became the first index fund investor by way of a lucky accident. Keith Shwayder, whose family had founded and owned Samsonite Luggage, was an assistant professor of accounting at the University of Chicago. Thus, he was exposed to the CAPM and the EMH, and he had a connection to a pension fund.

So where did things stand in 1971? The Markowitz framework had been around for almost 20 years, providing a general theory of portfolio selection. It didn't say anything about market efficiency. The following developments—the CAPM and the EMH—implied that active management was futile. This view came to dominate academic finance. With the increasing power of computers, these academic theories moved from abstractions to investible products. And the market crises of the early 1970s—including the oil embargo and the decline of the Nifty Fifty stocks—increased investor interest in new approaches to investing.

Active Management Strikes Back

The early 1970s saw an increasing disconnect between these academic theories, which favored indexing, and the actual practice of investing, which consisted almost entirely of active management at that time. Could active management utilize some of the advances in modern portfolio theory while retaining a belief that successful active management was possible?

Jack Treynor, Fischer Black, and Using Security Analysis to Improve Portfolio Selection. The first effort along these lines came from Jack Treynor and Fischer Black in 1973 when they published "How to Use Security Analysis to Improve Portfolio Selection." Treynor had been working on CAPM ideas around the same time as Sharpe, and Black was about to publish his paper with Myron Scholes on option pricing.[25] Treynor and Black (1973) tried to reconcile the advances in portfolio theory with the long history of security analysis. Even if most assets are efficiently priced, what should an investor do with information about some that may be inefficiently priced?

---

[25]Black and Scholes (1973).

They wrote, "We make the assumption that security analysis, properly used, can improve portfolio performance. This paper is directed toward finding a way to make the best possible use of the information provided by security analysts."[26]

Their mathematical analysis showed that investors should own the market portfolio *plus* an active (long–short) portfolio:

$$h_P(n) = h_{mkt}(n) + h_{PA}(n). \tag{3.13}$$

We can think of that active long–short portfolio as overweights and underweights relative to the market.[27] If security analysis provides little value, the investor will mainly hold the market portfolio. If security analysis does provide value, the investor will adjust the balance between the market and long–short portfolios accordingly. Using Sharpe's simplified model, Treynor and Black showed that the active position for each asset n, $h_{PA}(n)$, was proportional to the expected residual return (i.e., expected return beyond that implied by the CAPM) for that stock, α_n, divided by the variance of that residual return, ω_n^2:

$$\alpha_n = E\{\theta_n\}$$
$$\omega_n = StDev\{\theta_n\} \tag{3.14}$$
$$h_{PA}(n) \sim \frac{\alpha_n}{\omega_n^2}.$$

Note that in Equation 3.14, we use ω to denote residual risk—the standard deviation of the residual return, θ. We use σ to denote total risk—the standard deviation of the excess return, r.

Treynor and Black (1973) were not enthusiastically received by finance academics. They presented their paper at the CRSP (Center for Research in Security Prices) seminar at the University of Chicago in November 1967, and as Treynor recalled, "the talk did not go well."[28] They were presenting to academics who believed markets were efficient and active management was futile.

The contribution of Treynor and Black (1973) was to combine the CAPM with current practice into the overall Markowitz framework. It proposed the modern view that active management is difficult but not impossible and

---

[26]Treynor and Black (1973, p. 67).
[27]Note that Treynor and Black didn't require the portfolio to be long only.
[28]Mehrling (2005, p. 67).

that the Markowitz framework provides a systematic approach for active management.

Both Treynor and Black could have won Nobel Prizes, but neither did, for different reasons. Treynor had independently developed the ideas in the CAPM, which he circulated but never published. Black would certainly have won the Nobel Prize in Economic Sciences in 1997 with Myron Scholes and Robert Merton for their work on option pricing, but he died in 1995.

Fischer Black and Myron Scholes: From Theory to a New Financial Product. A second effort in support of active management came in 1974, when Fischer Black and Myron Scholes presented "From Theory to a New Financial Product" at the American Finance Association annual meeting. These two had published their option pricing paper (Black and Scholes 1973) the year before. In their 1974 paper, they described their efforts consulting for Wells Fargo Investment Advisors on a new product based on the latest financial theories. Although Black and Scholes (1974, p. 399) started with indexing, they did discuss some active management possibilities:

> The modern theory of finance suggests that most investors should put part or all of their money into a "market portfolio" mixed with borrowing or lending. Empirical evidence generally supports the theory, but there are some unanswered questions about the composition of the best market portfolio, and the apparent attractiveness of low risk stocks relative to high risk stocks, and about the ways of minimizing transaction costs. Attempts to create a fund based on these principles and to make it available to a large number of investors have uncovered some important problems. Legal costs due to government regulation, the costs of managing a fund, and especially the costs of selling it are all much higher than one might expect. Despite these problems, efforts to create such funds seem destined for eventual success.

They identified several interesting issues:

- How to choose the appropriate index

- The surprising attractiveness of low-volatility stocks, a potential active strategy[29]

- Real-world issues previously unexplored by academics: legal costs, government regulations, and costs of managing and selling a product

---

[29]The first published evidence for this effect—that low-beta stocks exhibit positive alphas and high-beta stocks exhibit negative alphas—was from Black, Jensen, and Scholes (1972). We now know this as the low-volatility factor used in today's smart beta products.

Black and Scholes (1974) made a few important contributions. Leading academics were applying the latest financial theory to develop an investable product, and their product mixed active and index components. As the authors noted, their product idea was marred by the difficulty they had in constructing and selling it. This paper went a step beyond Treynor and Black (1973) in providing rigorous empirical analysis leading to a proposed blend of attractive investment opportunities.

Barr Rosenberg and Factor Models of Portfolio Risk. The next development improved our understanding of risk by generalizing Sharpe's market model to more-versatile factor models. Sharpe identified one factor driving correlations between assets—the market. That model succeeded at simplifying calculations and made Markowitz optimization tractable for computers of that era, but it didn't accurately forecast risk. Although the market factor does explain a significant fraction of correlation, it misses important elements, as noted previously.

Barr Rosenberg (1974), a University of California, Berkeley, finance professor, generalized Sharpe's approach into a more flexible factor framework. Instead of one factor driving correlations, Rosenberg postulated many such factors—around 60—to capture the observed correlation structure in the US equity market:

$$r_n = \sum_{j=1}^{J} X_{nj} \cdot b_j + u_n. \tag{3.15}$$

Equation 3.15 states that the excess return to asset n consists of its exposures, X_{nj}, to a set of common factor returns, b_j, plus an idiosyncratic return, u_n, driven by issues specific to asset n.

For example, the excess return to ExxonMobil is due partly to the return to the oil industry, partly to returns to large stocks relative to small stocks, and partly to issues specific to ExxonMobil (e.g., the CEO's decision to retire and become US secretary of state). ExxonMobil is correlated with other stocks either because they are exposed to the same factors or because they are exposed to factors that are correlated. One key component of Rosenberg's factor model was that the idiosyncratic returns were uncorrelated: The model separated the common components of return from the idiosyncratic components.

Rosenberg's factor modeling approach added significant mathematical and computational complexity beyond Sharpe's model. It led to much more accurate forecasts of risk, but that wasn't sufficient to generate broad interest among investors. That interest followed from his choice of intuitive factors that resonated with them. Rosenberg's factors consisted of industries and investment styles (such as value and momentum).

Beyond writing a paper describing this approach, Rosenberg founded Barra, a company that provided factor models and associated analytics to investors. Investors didn't need to build their own factor models or run the calculations. They just needed to subscribe to Barra. Rosenberg was providing the tools of modern portfolio theory broadly to all investors.

Given the educational challenge of training investment managers to actually use modern portfolio theory, Barra started running annual seminars in Pebble Beach, California. In those early days, the seminars lasted four days and Rosenberg was the only speaker. I joined Barra in 1987—after Rosenberg had left Barra to start Rosenberg Institutional Equity Management (RIEM)—and by then, the seminars included talks by many different speakers (mainly Barra employees). The aura surrounding those conferences helped inspire the *Institutional Investor* magazine cover story in May 1978, "Who Is Barr Rosenberg and What the Hell Is He Talking About?"[30] The cover illustration shows Rosenberg sitting in a lotus position on a mountain top—wearing a flowing garment, with flowers in his hair—surrounded by (much smaller) genuflecting investment managers in suits and ties. Clearly, modern portfolio theory was becoming mainstream.

The factor models for risk developed by Barr Rosenberg made several contributions. They accurately forecasted risk, an improvement over the one-factor market model. They provided a coherent risk framework for investing, neatly organizing the various places that investors could try to outperform: betting on industries or factors, focusing on idiosyncratic (individual security) returns, or some blend of the two. The factor models simplified the calculations required by Markowitz optimization. Overall, Rosenberg accelerated the adoption of modern portfolio theory and, especially, placed risk at the center of investing.

The shortfall of Rosenberg's factor approach was its requirement that we identify all the common factors driving investment returns. It is not easy to do so.

Overall, Rosenberg's innovations had a huge impact on the investment business. They provided a compelling and usable risk framework for investors. They turned modern portfolio theory into a reality. And from small beginnings, trillions of dollars are now managed using factor models provided by Barra and its competitors.

---

[30]Welles (1978).

Stephen Ross and the Arbitrage Pricing Theory. Just as Barr Rosenberg had generalized Sharpe's market model to more accurate factor models of risk, in 1976, Stephen Ross generalized the CAPM, taking multiple factors into account in forecasting returns. His approach, the arbitrage pricing theory (APT), underlies today's increasingly popular smart beta/factor strategies.

Whereas Sharpe and the other developers of the CAPM assumed that all investors share the same assumptions and derived an equilibrium solution, Ross started with a factor model of risk and applied an approximate no-arbitrage condition.

Starting with the factor model (Equation 3.15) and the assumption that

$$\text{Corr}\{u_n, u_m\} = 0 \text{ for } n \neq m, \tag{3.16}$$

the arbitrage pricing theory states that

$$\text{E}\{u_n\} = 0. \tag{3.17}$$

This looks similar to the CAPM result that the expected residual return is zero, but the logic is quite different.

Here is the arbitrage argument: If $\text{E}\{u_n\} \neq 0$, then we could build a portfolio with positive expected return and *almost* zero risk. Because the specific returns are uncorrelated, we should be able to diversify away almost all the risk.

The other side of Ross's argument is that expected returns must connect to risk factors:

$$\text{E}\{r_n\} = \sum_{j=1}^{J} X_{nj} \cdot m_j, \tag{3.18}$$

where

$$m_j = \text{E}\{b_j\}. \tag{3.19}$$

Ross didn't specify the risk factors or say how to estimate their expected returns. But from the no-arbitrage condition, he showed that expected returns are related to risk factors.

The arbitrage pricing theory's contribution was to provide a detailed theory connecting expected returns directly to risk. It provided a flexible framework for estimating expected return. In terms of shortfalls, it was all theory, with little guidance on choosing factors. But—make no mistake—providing a risk-based framework for active management was a significant innovation.

Now the APT could be consistent with the CAPM if the expected factor returns were all proportional to their betas with respect to the market portfolio. But the APT didn't require that. In general, it offered a way of outperforming the market by choosing a more efficient mix of factors than that of the market portfolio. I believed Stephen Ross would win the Nobel Prize for this work, and Martin Leibowitz commented that he would have been one of the more deserving recipients, but unfortunately, Ross died before that could happen.

Daniel Kahneman and Amos Tversky on Psychology and Behavioral Finance. The APT arose out of advances in financial economics. The next development, behavioral finance, arose from a much less expected place: psychology.

Much of economic theory assumes that individuals are rational *utility maximizers*. That is, we all have utility functions that describe the value we receive for every possible activity and outcome, and we make all decisions so as to maximize our utility. That's clearly an approximation of reality; individuals aren't perfectly rational, after all. However, economists assumed that the deviations from rationality were random and would average out over larger populations.

Psychologists Daniel Kahneman and Amos Tversky (1979) showed that humans are not only irrational but *systematically* irrational. Their article "Prospect Theory: An Analysis of Decision under Risk" described how humans make predictable and repeatable mistakes. We can classify these mistakes into three categories[31]:

- Social interactions (conforming, follow-the-crowd behaviors)

- Heuristic simplification (generalizing from personal experience and recent events)

- Self-deception (overconfidence—e.g., attributing positive outcomes to skill and negative outcomes to luck)

Although Kahneman and Tversky developed and tested their ideas by observing human behaviors in the military and in psychology experiments conducted on undergraduates, the implications for investing are clear. For example, heuristic simplification (extrapolating from recent events) may explain why value stocks outperform growth stocks. Investors may incorrectly

---

[31]Hirshleifer (2001).

extrapolate recent earnings growth into the future, thereby overpricing growth stocks and underpricing value stocks.

This work led to Kahneman's Nobel Prize in Economic Sciences in 2002; Tversky would undoubtedly have shared that prize had he still been alive at the time. Michael Lewis's 2017 book *The Undoing Project* provides an insightful view into the relationship between these two very different people with very different backgrounds.

Kahneman and Tversky's work made several important contributions. Financial economics studies humans interacting in financial markets. Behavioral finance advances our understanding of human behavior in that endeavor. Critically important for active management, behavioral finance implies that successful active management is possible and points the way by identifying exploitable behaviors.

Behavioral finance also made an important contribution to academic finance, which in the years after the development of the CAPM and the EMH had evolved into a cult of market efficiency. Academics couldn't publish papers questioning market efficiency, and even pursuing research in that direction could threaten their careers. As academia slowly embraced behavioral finance, the inhibiting chains of market efficiency fell away.

Behavioral finance does have some shortcomings. First, with those undergraduate psychology experiments in mind, Mark Rubinstein (2001, p. 16) commented that the behavioral argument against rational markets "requires that we extrapolate from studies of *individual* decision makers done in narrow and restricted conditions to the complex and subtle environment of the security markets." Perhaps the behavioral biases uncovered by Kahneman and Tversky ring true as general observations of human behavior, but do they hold true in investment markets?

Second, another shortfall of behavioral finance is that it lacks a coherent overall framework, even almost 40 years after that first publication. It is a collection of interesting ideas rather than a coherent theory.

Third, regarding how investors have used behavioral finance, it has mainly provided *ex post* justification for effects we already knew about (e.g., that value stocks have outperformed growth stocks) rather than pointing toward previously undiscovered investment strategies.

Still, behavioral finance is one of the strongest arguments for the possibility of successful active management.

Sanford Grossman, Joseph Stiglitz, and Informationally Inefficient Markets. In 1980, Sanford Grossman and Joseph Stiglitz published a paper that supported successful active management and even argued that active management plays an important role in the economy by obtaining valuable information and helping set informed prices. In their article "On the Impossibility of Informationally Efficient Markets," they criticized the efficient market hypothesis by pointing out that because information is costly, market prices can't fully reflect all available information. If they did, then informed investors couldn't be compensated for their efforts to obtain that information. No investors would bother to become informed, and so prices couldn't reflect all available information.

Market prices can fully reflect all available information only in the special case where information is costless. However, obviously, information is not cost free. Also, more subtly, if information were costless, why even have secondary markets? We would know prices without the need for trading to convey information.

Grossman and Stiglitz (1980) helped active management strike back by pointing out a paradox at the heart of the efficient market hypothesis. Active managers must be compensated for their efforts in uncovering valuable intelligence.

Robert Shiller and Excess Volatility. Robert Shiller (1981) provided another compelling argument for the possibility of successful active management. He compared John Burr Williams's (1938) *Theory of Investment Value* with observed stock prices. If stock prices are predictions of discounted future cash flows, they should be less volatile than the actual discounted cash flows. But instead, they are *more* volatile. This excess volatility means that stocks are sometimes overpriced and sometimes underpriced. Although excess volatility doesn't point to any specific active strategy, it adds to the arguments that successful active management is possible. Thanks to Shiller, we know that stocks are often mispriced. Shiller shared the 2013 Nobel Prize in Economic Sciences for this work.

The Evolution of Investing

Over the past 100 years or so, investing has evolved from a few rules of thumb based on poor or nonexistent data to a world increasingly dominated by theory and systematic approaches. Active management still dominates, but investors now understand it as a bet against the benchmark of indexing. And indexing and systematic active management are both increasingly popular.

Appendix

In preparing the material in this chapter and presenting it to audiences at Stellenbosch University and the London Quant Group Oxford seminar, as well as at BlackRock, I received many suggestions of important intellectual milestones to include. I have included some of those suggestions but chose to leave out many more—not because they didn't represent important break-throughs, but because, in my opinion, they were not sufficiently central to the development of investment management. Those developments include the following:

- James Tobin's mutual fund separation theory, on which he published an article in the *Review of Economic Studies* in 1958. It showed that just two efficient frontier portfolios span the entire efficient frontier—that is, we can achieve the expected return and risk of any point on the efficient frontier as a combination of any two specific portfolios on the efficient frontier.

- Alfred Winslow Jones's concept of "relative velocity," which he described in a 1961 report to his investors—a precursor to market beta that allowed him to manage the world's first hedge fund.

- Edward Thorp's *Beat the Market*, published in 1967. This book made use of the Kelly criterion, developed by J.L. Kelly, Jr., in 1956, to determine the bet size needed to maximize growth in wealth.

- Milgrom and Stokey's 1982 article "Information, Trade and Common Knowledge." It argues that one trader receiving private information will not create incentives to trade when everyone has rational expectations.

Bibliography

Ancell, Kate. 2012. "The Origin of the First Index Fund." University of Chicago Booth School of Business publication (28 March). https://research.chicagobooth.edu/fama-miller/docs/the-origin-of-the-first-index-fund.pdf.

Bernstein, Peter L. 1992. *Capital Ideas: The Improbable Origins of Modern Wall Street*, 2nd ed. New York: Free Press.

———. 2007. *Capital Ideas Evolving*. Hoboken: John Wiley & Sons, Inc.

Black, Fischer, Michael C. Jensen, and Myron Scholes. 1972. "The Capital Asset Pricing Model: Some Empirical Tests." In *Studies in the Theory of Capital Markets*, edited by Michael C. Jensen, 249–65. New York: Praeger.

Black, Fischer, and Myron Scholes. 1973. "The Pricing of Options and Corporate Liabilities." *Journal of Political Economy* 81 (3): 637–654.

————. 1974. "From Theory to a New Financial Product." *Journal of Finance* 29 (2): 399–412.

Fama, Eugene F. 1970. "Efficient Capital Markets: A Review of Theory and Empirical Work." *Journal of Finance* 25 (2): 383–417.

Goetzmann, William N. 2016. *Money Changes Everything: How Finance Made Civilization Possible*. Princeton, NJ: Princeton University Press.

Graham, Benjamin. 1973. *The Intelligent Investor*, 4th ed. New York: Harper.

Graham, Benjamin, and David L. Dodd. 2009. *Security Analysis*, 6th ed. New York: McGraw-Hill.

Grinold, Richard C., and Ronald N. Kahn. 2000. *Active Portfolio Management*, 2nd ed. New York: McGraw-Hill.

Grossman, Sanford J., and Joseph E. Stiglitz. 1980. "On the Impossibility of Informationally Efficient Markets." *American Economic Review* 70 (3): 393–408.

Hirshleifer, David. 2001. "Investor Psychology and Asset Pricing." *Journal of Finance* 56 (4): 1533–97.

Jahnke, William W. 1990. "The Development of Structured Portfolio Management: A Contextual View." In *Quantitative International Investing: A Handbook of Analytical and Methodological Techniques and Strategies*, edited by Brian Bruce, 153–81. New York: McGraw-Hill.

Jones, A.W. 1961. "Basic Report to the Limited Partners." Described in valuewalk.com/2016/05/a-w-jones-letters/.

Kahneman, Daniel, and Amos Tversky. 1979. "Prospect Theory: An Analysis of Decision under Risk." *Econometrica* 47 (2): 263–91.

Kelly, J.L. 1956. "A New Interpretation of Information Rate." *Bell System Technical Journal* 35 (4): 917–26.

Lewis, Michael. 2017. *The Undoing Project: A Friendship That Changed Our Minds*. New York: W.W. Norton & Company.

Lintner, John. 1965. "The Valuation of Risk Assets and the Selection of Risky Investments in Stock Portfolios and Capital Budgets." *Review of Economics and Statistics* 47 (1): 13–37.

Lowenfeld, Henry. 1909. *Investment: An Exact Science*. London: Financial Review of Reviews.

Markowitz, Harry. 1952. "Portfolio Selection." *Journal of Finance* 7 (1): 77–91.

———. 1990. "Foundations of Portfolio Theory." Nobel Lecture (7 December).

Mehrling, Perry. 2005. *Fischer Black and the Revolutionary Idea of Finance.* Hoboken, NJ: John Wiley & Sons.

Milgrom, Paul, and Nancy Stokey. 1982. "Information, Trade and Common Knowledge." *Journal of Economic Theory* 26 (1): 17–27.

Mossin, Jan. 1966. "Equilibrium in a Capital Asset Market." *Econometrica* 34 (4): 768–83.

Niederhoffer, Victor. 1997. *The Education of a Speculator.* New York: John Wiley & Sons.

Rosenberg, Barr. 1974. "Extra-Market Components of Covariance in Security Markets." *Journal of Financial and Quantitative Analysis* 9 (2): 263–74.

Ross, Stephen A. 1976. "The Arbitrage Theory of Capital Asset Pricing." *Journal of Economic Theory* 13 (3): 341–60.

Rubinstein, Mark. 2001. "Rational Markets: Yes or No? The Affirmative Case." *Financial Analysts Journal* 57 (3): 15–29.

———. 2006. *A History of the Theory of Investments.* Hoboken, NJ: John Wiley & Sons.

Sharpe, William F. 1963. "A Simplified Model for Portfolio Analysis." *Management Science* 9 (2): 277–93.

———. 1964. "Capital Asset Prices: A Theory of Market Equilibrium under Conditions of Risk." *Journal of Finance* 19 (3): 425–42.

Shiller, Robert. 1981. "Do Stock Prices Move Too Much to Be Justified by Subsequent Changes in Dividends?" *American Economic Review* 71 (3): 421–36.

Thorp, Edward. 1967. *Beat the Market: A Scientific Stock Market System.* New York: Random House.

Tobin, James. 1958. "Liquidity Preference as Behavior towards Risk." *Review of Economic Studies* 25 (1): 65–86.

Treynor, Jack. 1961. "Toward a Theory of the Market Value of Risky Assets." Unpublished manuscript.

Treynor, Jack L., and Fischer Black. 1973. "How to Use Security Analysis to Improve Portfolio Selection." *Journal of Business* 46 (1): 66–86.

Welles, Chris. 1978. "Who Is Barr Rosenberg and What the Hell Is He Talking About?" *Institutional Investor* (May): 59-66.

Williams, John Burr. 1938. *The Theory of Investment Value*. Cambridge, MA: Harvard University Press.

4. Seven Insights into Active Management

Give me insight into today, and you may have the antique and future worlds.

—*Ralph Waldo Emerson*

By the early 1970s, a number of academic developments held out hope for the possibility of successful active management. In this chapter, I delve in more mathematical detail into seven insights that emerged in roughly the following 20-year period. Some of these ideas appeared in well-known papers, my book with Richard Grinold, *Active Portfolio Management*, and in the 1999 summary, *Seven Quantitative Insights into Active Management*, published by Barra (now MSCI) and Barclays Global Investors (now BlackRock).[32] This chapter is a bit more mathematical than the prior chapters focused on history, though a basic understanding of these insights will not require too much math. And this chapter builds on mathematical concepts introduced already. The chapter also provides a detailed view into systematic thinking about active management.

When I discussed Treynor and Black's work on using security analysis to improve portfolio selection, I introduced alpha as forecast residual return. The capital asset pricing model states that the expected residual return is zero. However, the active manager, having identified some useful information, forecasts residual returns not equal to zero. Much of the job of an active manager is to forecast residual returns. Active managers can also forecast market returns, and some do. As I show in this chapter, however, it's difficult to deliver consistent performance by implementing such forecasts (timing the market). Note that active managers and investors use the term *alpha* for several different things: forecast or realized residual or active return (where active return is simply the return minus the benchmark return).[33] I consistently use alpha to denote *forecast residual* returns. If I need to discuss any of its other meanings, I explicitly clarify them. Treynor and Black connected the forecast alphas to portfolio positions. I presented their final result, though not the analysis. For the purposes of this chapter, I need to connect forecast residual returns with optimal portfolios. I do this via Markowitz mean–variance optimization. Given our alpha forecasts and risk forecasts for any possible

---

[32]Grinold and Kahn (2000); Kahn (1999).

[33]The difference between active return and residual return may be thought of as follows: Active return is simply the arithmetic difference between the return on an asset or portfolio and that of its benchmark. To calculate the residual return, one *leverages the benchmark* up or down to match the beta risk of the asset or portfolio and then calculates the difference.

portfolio, we can find the portfolio that achieves the highest expected alpha for any given risk level. In particular, I define utility as follows:

$$\text{Utility} = \mathbf{h}^T \cdot \boldsymbol{\alpha} - \lambda \mathbf{h}^T \cdot \mathbf{V} \cdot \mathbf{h}$$
$$= \alpha_p - \lambda \omega_p^2. \tag{4.1}$$

In Equation 4.1, $\mathbf{h}$ is the vector of portfolio holdings, $\boldsymbol{\alpha}$ is the vector of forecast alphas, $\mathbf{V}$ is the covariance matrix for the assets, λ is the risk-aversion parameter capturing investor preferences, and ω measures risk.

We choose the portfolio that maximizes utility. To do that, we take the derivative of the utility with respect to each of the holdings and set those equal to zero. For the optimal portfolio, Q,

$$\boldsymbol{\alpha} = 2\lambda \mathbf{V} \cdot \mathbf{h}_Q. \tag{4.2}$$

Equation 4.2 directly connects our forecast alphas to portfolio positions. As we vary the risk-aversion parameter, λ, the optimal portfolio will vary. The overweights and underweights (or long positions and short positions) will scale up and down. In this way, the optimal portfolio risk will vary with risk aversion.

Insight 1. Active Management Is a Zero-Sum Game

William F. Sharpe published "The Arithmetic of Active Management" in 1991. It is a two-page paper containing no equations whatsoever. In it, he makes a simple argument:

- The sum of all active management and index management positions is the market.

- The sum of all index management positions is the market.

- Hence, the sum of all active management positions is the market.

Based on this simple argument that active management in aggregate sums to the market, Sharpe concluded that the (asset-weighted) *average* active manager matches the market's performance before fees and costs. This is true whether or not the market is efficient. So, after fees and costs, the average active manager must underperform the market. Index funds are above-median performers, once again independent of whether the market is efficient.

Sharpe's argument is quite powerful, though he does make a few assumptions. He assumes that all index management positions sum to the market. This assumption isn't exactly true even for just the broad market index funds, because those funds are often managed to different indexes. In the United States, we have broad market index funds managed against the S&P 500, the Russell 1000 Index, and the MSCI USA Index—not to mention broad market small-cap indexes. There are also sector and other not-broad index funds whose positions wouldn't necessarily sum to the market. On the active management side, professional active managers are trying to outperform market indexes. There are also investors who hold non-market-cap-weighted portfolios (which are active because they differ from the market) but who are not professional active managers. These investors hold positions, often with little active trading, either because their holdings might be part of executive compensation, because trading would trigger significant capital gains, or for other reasons.

Still, considerable empirical evidence supports the key implication of Sharpe's arithmetic of active management: that the average active manager underperforms the market. For example, Eugene Fama and Kenneth French (2010) showed that active US equity mutual funds have produced a realized alpha of roughly zero on average before fees over the period from 1984 through 2006. They estimated the average realized alpha after fees to be somewhere between −0.81% and −1.13% per year, with the exact number depending on whether they control for one, three, or four factors. My definition of alpha controls for only one factor—the market (or a broad market index)—but Fama and French also controlled for size and value factors and in their four-factor analysis, momentum.

There are at least three important implications of the arithmetic of active management. First, tests of whether successful active management is possible need to look beyond average active performance. We know that the average active manager will underperform every year, even if few successful active managers outperform year after year. Relatedly, if you want to become an active manager, it's not good enough to be average. You need to believe that you can consistently be a top-quartile active manager.

The second implication is that broad market index funds will be consistent second-quartile (or at least above-median) performers. This performance is independent of the efficiency of the market, and it provides a strong argument in favor of indexing. Unless the investor has the ability to identify successful active managers, he is better off with indexing. Otherwise, he is randomly choosing managers with negative expected alpha.

The third implication is that the burden of proof is on active managers to demonstrate that their expected active returns will more than compensate for added risk and cost.

Insight 2. Information Ratios Determine Added Value

Let's focus on the active manager's job: outperforming a benchmark. Active managers build portfolios by trading off alpha against residual risk (denoted by ω and shortened to simply "risk" in this discussion). As noted previously, the utility, or added value, from active management is given in Equation 4.1.

Individual preferences enter into the utility only in how individuals trade off residual return against risk. More risk-averse investors will demand more incremental return for each unit of risk.

The information ratio is the manager's ratio of residual return to risk:

$$IR_P = \frac{\alpha_P}{\omega_P}. \tag{4.3}$$

We will consider this a fundamental constant defining the manager, assuming it does not vary with time or the level of risk. A manager can deliver more residual return only by taking on more risk:

$$\alpha_P = IR_P \cdot \omega_P. \tag{4.4}$$

This assertion is exactly true in the absence of constraints. For example, if the manager overweights one position by 5% and underweights another by 3%, leading to a given forecast alpha, she can double both the alpha and the risk by increasing the overweight to 10% and the underweight to 6%.

Understanding Information Ratios. We can think of the information ratio as a measure of *consistency* of performance—that is, the probability that the manager will realize positive residual returns every period. **Exhibit 4.1** shows the probability distribution of annual alphas for three different information ratio distributions.

In this simple illustration, all three distributions have a residual risk level of 2% and the residual returns are normally distributed. As the information ratio increases, the distribution simply shifts to the right. The probability of realizing a positive residual return is simply the area under the curve to the right of $\alpha = 0$. This probability strictly increases in this example as the information ratio increases.

Even if we are comparing distributions with differing risk levels, if the residual returns are normally distributed, we find that the probability of realizing a positive residual return over one year is

$$\Pr\{\alpha > 0\} = \Phi\{IR\}, \tag{4.5}$$

Exhibit 4.1.   Alpha Distributions

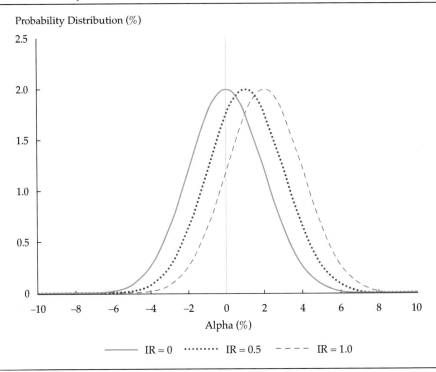

where Φ is the cumulative normal distribution function. At least in the normal distribution case, the consistency of performance is a monotonic function of the information ratio: The higher the information ratio, the more likely it is that the manager will realize positive residual return in any period. Although residual returns are not exactly normally distributed, we do generally observe that consistency of performance increases with information ratios.

Utility Analysis. Using Equation 4.4, we can rewrite the utility (i.e., the added value) as

$$\text{Utility} = IR_p \cdot \omega_p - \lambda \omega_p^2. \tag{4.6}$$

Exhibit 4.2 shows graphically how utility depends on risk. The active manager chooses the portfolio corresponding to the maximum point in Exhibit 4.2. At this point,

$$\omega^* = \frac{IR_p}{2\lambda}. \tag{4.7}$$

Exhibit 4.2. Utility as a Function of Risk

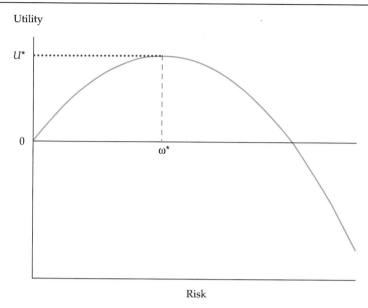

$$U^* = \frac{(IR_P)^2}{4\lambda}.$$ (4.8)

Equation 4.7 describes the optimal level of residual risk, ω^*. Optimal residual risk depends inversely on risk aversion and directly on the information ratio. More-risk-averse investors will choose lower levels of residual risk. The higher the information ratio—and as we have seen, the higher the consistency of performance—the more residual risk an investor will tolerate.

Each investor's maximum added value depends, according to Equation 4.8, directly on the square of the information ratio and inversely on the risk aversion. This is the critical point. It means that a very risk-averse investor, one with a very high value of λ, will maximize added value by investing with the manager with the highest information ratio. But a risk-tolerant investor, with a low value of λ, will reach exactly the same conclusion. The only difference between the two is how much they will invest with that manager versus an index fund, the zero-residual-risk choice.

All investors, regardless of their preferences, will agree that the highest information ratio can provide the most value. Equation 4.8 shows that information ratios determine added value.

Typical Values for Information Ratios. Given the central role of information ratios, it is useful to know their typical values. Based on research at Barra and BlackRock, the typical before-expenses distribution of information ratios is shown in **Exhibit 4.3**, and specific empirical results are shown in **Exhibit 4.4**.

Exhibit 4.3 shows the typical distribution numbers. A top-quartile manager can add 50 bps of realized residual return for every 100 bps of residual risk, before expenses. This finding holds for both equity and fixed-income funds. Exhibit 4.4 shows results for studies of US equity mutual funds and institutional portfolios, and fixed-income institutional portfolios over the five-year period from 2003 through 2007. These studies used Sharpe (1992) style analysis to separate style from selection return for each fund. The style

Exhibit 4.3. Typical Distribution of Information Ratios

Percentile	IR	$Pr\{\alpha > 0\}$
90	1.0	84%
75	0.5	69
50	0.0	50
25	−0.5	31
10	−1.0	16

Source: Grinold and Kahn (2000).

Exhibit 4.4. Information Ratio Empirical Results

	Information Ratios				
	Equity			Fixed Income	
Percentile	Mutual Funds	Long-Only Inst.	Long–Short Inst.	Institutional	Average
90	1.04	0.77	1.17	0.96	0.99
75	0.64	0.42	0.57	0.5	0.53
50	0.2	0.02	0.25	0.01	0.12
25	−0.21	−0.38	−0.22	−0.45	−0.32
10	−0.62	−0.77	−0.58	−0.9	−0.72

Notes: These results are for US data over the five-year period from January 2003 through December 2007. Empirical studies included 338 equity mutual funds, 1,679 equity long-only institutional funds, 56 equity long–short institutional funds, and 537 fixed-income mutual funds.
Source: BlackRock.

component of the return represents the effective benchmark of each fund. Exhibit 4.3 shows information ratios of the selection returns. Exact results will vary with the historical period, the asset class under review, and the methodology. These empirical results are roughly consistent with the data in Exhibit 4.3.

Insight 3. Allocate Risk Budget in Proportion to Information Ratios

Insight 2 showed that investors should choose active managers on the basis of their information ratios. What should an investor do when confronted with many investment choices, with a variety of information ratios? The investor will find the highest-information-ratio manager the most attractive, but should the investor place all his money with that manager?

We can also analyze this situation with mean–variance optimization. Let's say the investor has identified N different managers, each offering a particular expected alpha, α_n, at residual risk ω_n and hence information ratio IR_n. For simplicity, assume that these managers' residual returns are all uncorrelated. We don't need to make this assumption, but it simplifies the analytical results.

The investor places a fraction h_n with each manager. The portfolio alpha and risk are

$$\alpha_P = \sum_{n=1}^{N} h_n \cdot \alpha_n. \tag{4.9}$$

$$\omega_P^2 = \sum_{n=1}^{N} h_n^2 \cdot \omega_n^2. \tag{4.10}$$

The investor chooses allocations to maximize her utility. The results are

$$h_n^* = \frac{\alpha_n}{2\lambda\omega_n^2} \Rightarrow \frac{IR_n}{2\lambda\omega_n}. \tag{4.11}$$

$$h_n^* \cdot \omega_n = \frac{IR_n}{2\lambda}. \tag{4.12}$$

Equation 4.11 shows that the investor optimally allocates capital in proportion to information ratios divided by risk. But, perhaps more naturally, Equation 4.12 shows that the investor allocates risk in proportion to information ratios. The quantity $h_n^* \cdot \omega_n$ is the investor's capital allocation times the risk, which is the *risk allocation*. It measures how much risk the investment contributes at the portfolio level. For example, if the investor places 20% of the capital in a fund with 5% risk, that allocation contributes 1% risk at the portfolio level.

The key observation here: Investors allocate risk in proportion to information ratios.[34] The investor does not allocate all the capital, and all the risk, to the best manager—that is, the manager with the highest information ratio. She allocates the most risk to that manager but still diversifies among other managers because she does not know which manager will have the best performance after the fact; the information ratio is just an expectation, not a guarantee, of performance.

Insight 4. Alphas Must Control for Skill, Volatility, and Expectations

This insight shows how to process raw information into alphas, which are critical inputs for active management.

Raw signals, such as analyst earnings forecasts, broker buy/sell recommendations, and the number of cars in a Walmart parking lot the week before Christmas, hopefully contain information useful in forecasting returns. But these raw data are not alphas (expected residual returns). They are not even necessarily denominated in units of return.

A basic forecasting formula governs the connection between these raw signals and alphas. This formula refines the raw signals into alphas by controlling for expectations, skill, and volatility. In many cases, we can simplify this formula to a particularly intuitive form.

The basic forecasting formula provides the best linear unbiased estimate (BLUE) of the residual return, θ, given the raw signal, g:

$$E\{\theta \mid g\} = E\{\theta\} + \text{Cov}\{\theta, g\} \cdot \text{Var}^{-1}\{g\} \cdot [g - E\{g\}]. \tag{4.13}$$

According to Equation 4.13, the expected residual return conditional on g equals the unconditional expected residual return plus a term that depends

---

[34]For those worried about our assumption that these investment choices are uncorrelated, if we take correlations into account, we find that

$$\mathbf{h} \cdot \omega = \frac{\rho^{-1} \cdot \mathbf{IR}}{2\lambda}.$$

Here, $\mathbf{h}$ is the vector of capital allocations, ω is a diagonal matrix with residual risks on the diagonal, ρ is the correlation matrix, and $\mathbf{IR}$ is a vector of information ratios.

on the difference between the observed signal and its unconditional expectation. Reordering terms, we see that

$$E\{\theta \,|\, g\} - E\{\theta\} \equiv \alpha = \text{Cov}\{\theta, g\} \cdot \text{Var}^{-1}\{g\} \cdot [g - E\{g\}]. \qquad (4.14)$$

As discussed at the beginning of this chapter, the unconditional expected residual return is zero, and alpha is the expected residual return conditional on the manager's information, g.

This formula controls for expectations. Only if g differs from its unconditional expectation will the expected residual return differ from its unconditional expectation. Put another way, only if g differs from its unconditional expectation will the expected alpha differ from zero.

This result is intuitive. If company earnings exactly match expectations, we do not expect the stock to move. Movement happens only when earnings do not match expectations.

Now let's simplify Equation 4.14 into a more intuitive form that reveals how alphas include controls for skill and volatility. The definitions of variance and covariance tell us the following:

$$\text{Var}\{g\} = [\text{StDev}\{g\}]^2. \qquad (4.15)$$

$$\text{Cov}\{\theta, g\} = \text{Corr}\{\theta, g\} \cdot \text{StDev}\{\theta\} \cdot \text{StDev}\{g\}. \qquad (4.16)$$

Substituting Equations 4.15 and 4.16 into Equation 4.14 leads to

$$\alpha = \text{Corr}\{\theta, g\} \cdot \text{StDev}\{\theta\} \cdot \left[\frac{g - E\{g\}}{\text{StDev}\{g\}} \right]. \qquad (4.17)$$

We commonly refer to the correlation of the signal and the subsequent realization as the *information coefficient* (IC), and the standard deviation of the residual return is the residual risk (ω). We refer to the standardized raw signal as a z-score, or score for short, because by construction it has a mean of 0 and a standard deviation of 1. If the z-scores are normally distributed or close to normally distributed, then about 95% of the time z will range from −2 to +2. That is usually the case, but we will not assume that it is always true. Putting this together, we get

$$\alpha = IC \cdot \omega \cdot z. \qquad (4.18)$$

We have decomposed alpha into three components: an information coefficient, a volatility, and a score.

Equation 4.18 clearly shows how alphas control for skill, volatility, and expectations. The information coefficient is a measure of skill. With no skill—that is, no correlation between signal and subsequent return—the information coefficient is zero and Equation 4.18 sets the alpha to zero, as it should. The greater the skill, the greater the alpha, other things equal.

Understanding Skill. It is useful to provide some context for this important measure of skill. First, **Exhibit 4.5** shows the range of typical information coefficients.

These correlations are small. Consistent with the arithmetic of active management, the average information coefficient is zero. But even a great information coefficient is only 0.1. We know that, as a correlation, the maximum possible information coefficient is 1. But these numbers are much lower than that. Forecasting residual returns is difficult. To better understand these magnitudes, we can relate the information coefficient to a simpler measure of skill: how often the manager correctly forecasts the sign of the residual return. If the manager gets the sign right only 50% of the time, he doesn't have skill. If we assume that residual returns and forecast errors are normally distributed and that the information coefficient is much less than 1, we find that the fraction of times the manager correctly forecasts the sign is

$$
\begin{aligned}
fr &= \left(\frac{1}{2}\right) + \left(\frac{1}{\pi}\right) \cdot \text{Arctan}\left\{\frac{IC}{\sqrt{1-IC^2}}\right\} \\
&\approx \left(\frac{1}{2}\right) + \left(\frac{IC}{\pi}\right) \text{ for } IC \ll 1.
\end{aligned}
\tag{4.19}
$$

We can see more explicitly that if the information coefficient is zero, the manager correctly forecasts the sign of the residual return 50% of the time. But as the information coefficient increases, the manager correctly forecasts the sign more than 50% of the time. **Exhibit 4.6** expands Exhibit 4.5 to convert information coefficients into probabilities of forecasting the correct sign.

Exhibit 4.6 and Equation 4.19 help us understand how difficult it is to correctly forecast residual returns. An exceptional information coefficient of

Exhibit 4.5. Typical Information Coefficients

Skill	IC
Average	0.00
Good	0.05
Great	0.10

Exhibit 4.6.   Probability of Forecasting the Correct Sign

Skill	IC	fr
Average	0.00	50.0%
Good	0.05	51.6
Great	0.10	53.2

0.1 corresponds to correctly forecasting the sign of the residual return about 53% of the time. I soon show that the key to turning that small edge in each investment decision into a high information ratio is diversification.

Volatility serves two purposes in Equation 4.18. First, it causes the forecast alpha to be expressed in units of return. The information coefficient and the score are dimensionless. Second, it controls the alpha for volatility. For a given skill level, imagine two stocks with equally bullish scores of +1. We believe both stocks will go up. Equation 4.18 says that the higher-volatility stock will go up more. If both a low-volatility utility stock and a high-volatility technology stock achieve earnings one standard deviation above expectations, the technology stock should rise more. Both stocks will rise, but the technology stock will rise more than the utility stock.

Keep in mind that optimal holdings are roughly proportional to alpha divided by residual variance. Even if we give the more volatile stock the higher alpha, it will receive a smaller position. The amount of risk we take in each position, though, is proportional to the score.

The score implements the control for expectations because it has an expectation of zero. Only when the signal doesn't match expectations does the score differ from zero.

Understanding the three constituent parts of an alpha can inform our intuition. It can also provide structure in unstructured situations, where the connections between raw signals and alphas are unclear.

Examples. The ultimate example of an unstructured situation is a stock tip. Even in this case, Equation 4.18 can provide structure. Imagine that the stock in question has a residual volatility of 20%. **Exhibit 4.7** shows the range of possible alphas as a function of the information coefficient and score.

Because stock tips are always presented as very, very positive ("I make only one or two recommendations a year, and you are the first person I called …"), converting from the tip to an alpha requires only estimating the tipper's information coefficient. Ask yourself, Is Warren Buffett on the line, or is it someone you have never heard of?

Exhibit 4.7. Alpha of a Stock Tip

IC	Very Positive: $z = 1$	Very, Very Positive: $z = 2$
Great: 0.10	2	4%
Good: 0.05	1	2
Average: 0.0	0	0

Exhibit 4.8. Broker Buy/Sell Alphas: Information Coefficient of 0.05

ω	View	Score	Alpha
15%	Buy	1	0.75%
20%	Buy	1	1.00
15%	Sell	−1	−0.75
30%	Buy	1	1.50
25%	Sell	−1	−1.25

For an institutional money manager, a more relevant example involves converting broker buy/sell recommendations into alphas. This common situation has relatively little structure, but understanding alphas can help. **Exhibit 4.8** shows an example, assuming that the broker has a good information coefficient of 0.05.

Our conversion from recommendations to scores is straightforward. Notice that the first two stocks in the list, both recommended, have different alphas. We expect the second stock, with a higher volatility, to go up more than the first stock. Contrast this with simply giving every stock on the buy list an alpha of 1%. If all the buy recommendations have the same expected returns, an optimizer would choose the minimum-risk portfolio of those buy recommendations—loading up on the least volatile stocks.

Insight 5. The Fundamental Law of Active Management: Information Ratios Depend on Skill, Diversification, and Efficiency

Previously, we learned that the information ratio is the key to active management. Given that fact, how can we achieve high information ratios? Let's begin by looking at a relationship Richard Grinold first described in 1989 as the "Fundamental Law of Active Management." This law expresses the information ratio in terms of three other statistics—the information coefficient, a measure of skill; breadth, a measure of diversification; and the transfer coefficient, a measure of efficiency of implementation:[35]

$$IR = IC \cdot \sqrt{BR} \cdot TC. \tag{4.20}$$

We previously examined the information coefficient in detail, and we know that it measures skill. If the information coefficient is zero, no correlation exists between a manager's forecasts and the subsequent realizations, and the manager's information ratio is zero.

Understanding Breadth. Breadth—really breadth *of skill*—measures the number of independent bets the manager takes per year at an average skill level of *IC*. It measures diversification. We define breadth as bets per year because we define the information ratio as an annualized quantity.

According to the fundamental law, to achieve a high information ratio, a manager must demonstrate an edge in making individual investment decisions and then diversify that edge over many separate decisions. But breadth is still a measure of the diversity of decisions to which the manager has skill to apply. The fundamental law does not say that there is any advantage to investing in asset classes about which the manager knows nothing.

Breadth is the part of the fundamental law that is hardest to understand. As the number of independent bets per year, it is a rate, not a number. It's not the number of assets in the portfolio. We expect twice as many bets over two years than one year, so the number of holdings isn't the right concept.

To provide some additional insight into breadth, consider an investment process in equilibrium. Old information decays as new information arrives. In equilibrium, the two are in balance, and so the information turnover rate, γ, captures both the decay rate of old information and the arrival rate of new information. We can capture this situation schematically with Equation 4.21:

$$\alpha_n(t) = e^{-\gamma \cdot \Delta t} \cdot \alpha_n(t - \Delta t) + \tilde{s}_n(t). \tag{4.21}$$

Equation 4.21 shows that old information decays over time and new information, $\tilde{s}_n(t)$, arrives over time. Equation 4.21 implies that the decay and arrival of information happen somewhat continuously, which isn't usually true. It does show how old information (last period's alpha forecast) decays over time while new information keeps arriving. Assuming that these two

---

[35]Grinold (1989) included only the first two terms, effectively assuming perfect implementation. Clarke, de Silva, and Thorley (2002) extended the fundamental law, adding the transfer coefficient to account for imperfect implementation.

processes are in balance, we can show that the breadth of this forecast is

$$BR = \gamma \cdot N. \tag{4.22}$$

Equation 4.22 shows how the breadth relates to both the number of assets under consideration and the information turnover rate.[36]

This result is useful. Given a signal for N assets over time, we can estimate the coefficient, γ, using Equation 4.21 and then estimate breadth via Equation 4.22. For example, if we run a cross-sectional regression of $\alpha(t)$ against $\alpha(t - \Delta t)$, we can estimate $e^{-\gamma \cdot \Delta t}$ as a regression coefficient.

As a particular example, imagine we follow 300 stocks and every week we receive new information on 12 of those stocks. We don't know ahead of time which 12 stocks the new information will cover. Our breadth is $12 \times 52 = 624$.

But we could also represent this information process as

$$\alpha_n(t) = \begin{bmatrix} \text{No change,} & p = \left(\dfrac{288}{300}\right) \\ \text{New information,} & p = \left(\dfrac{12}{300}\right) \end{bmatrix}. \tag{4.23}$$

Because we cannot predict the new information, our expected alphas become

$$E\{\alpha_n(t)\} = \left(\frac{288}{300}\right) \cdot \alpha_n(t - \Delta t). \tag{4.24}$$

But comparing Equations 4.24 and 4.21 leads us to estimate

$$\gamma \cdot \Delta t \approx \left(\frac{12}{300}\right) \tag{4.25}$$

$$\gamma \cdot N \Rightarrow 12 \cdot 52 = 624.$$

The mathematical formalism of Equation 4.21 leads back to the intuitive answer.

Non-Investment Example. Before considering the third term in the fundamental law, the transfer coefficient, let's consider a non-investment example of the law: the roulette wheel. The American roulette wheel includes the numbers 1 through 36, 0, and 00. Consider players betting that the roulette number will be even. The players win if the number is 2, 4, 6, …, 36. The casino wins if the number is 1, 3, 5, …, 35. The casino has a small edge because it also

---

[36]See Grinold and Kahn (2011) for details.

Exhibit 4.9. $2.5 Million Bet on One Spin of the Wheel

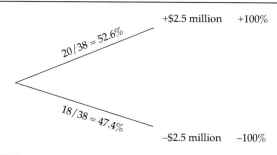

wins if the final number is 0 or 00. The roulette wheel can stop at 38 possible numbers. The player wins if 18 of those numbers come up. The casino wins if 20 of those numbers come up. Now imagine that during the course of the year, players bet a total of $2.5 million on this roulette wheel. Consider two possible scenarios. In the first scenario, the players all agree to pool resources and bet all $2.5 million on one spin of the wheel. In the second, that $2.5 million consists of 100,000 spins of the wheel with a $25 bet on each spin.

Exhibit 4.9 shows the first scenario, from the casino's perspective. The casino has a 52.6% chance of winning $2.5 million and a 47.4% chance of losing $2.5 million. Let's analyze this situation in a bit more detail. View the forecasts as ±1 and the realized returns as ±100%.

We start with the casino's expected return and variance of return:

$$E\{r\} = 0.526(100\%) + 0.474(-100\%) = 5.2\%. \tag{4.26}$$

$$\begin{aligned} \text{Var}\{r\} &= 0.526(100\% - 5.2\%)^2 + 0.474(-100\% - 5.2\%)^2 \\ &= (99.9\%)^2. \end{aligned} \tag{4.27}$$

The casino's expected return is 5.2%, and the standard deviation of the return is 99.9%. In dollar terms, the casino's expected winning is $130,000, with a standard deviation of almost $2.5 million. The notably high standard deviation isn't surprising because the casino faces only two possible outcomes—up 100% or down 100%—with the positive outcome only slightly more likely.

We can also calculate the casino's information coefficient. It is positive because it forecasts winning, and the casino does win 52.6% of the time:

$$\text{Cov}\{r, g\} = E\{r \cdot g\} = 0.526(+1) + 0.474(-1) = 0.052 \tag{4.28}$$
$$IC = 5.2\%.$$

In this simple case, the variances of r and g are almost exactly 1, so the covariance and the correlation are effectively the same.[37]

We can now check out the fundamental law of active management. We can calculate the information ratio directly on the basis of our calculations of the casino's expected return and its standard deviation. We can then compare it to the fundamental law result, with a breadth of 1 for this scenario.

$$IR = \frac{5.2\%}{99.9\%} = 0.052 = IC \cdot \sqrt{BR}. \tag{4.29}$$

The information ratio is quite low, yet the information coefficient looks good from the perspective of active management. The problem is that the breadth is very low. It is not surprising that casinos do not encourage this approach to roulette.

The analysis of the second, more standard scenario is somewhat similar. In this case, though, we play the game 100,000 times over the course of the year and assume each game involves 1/100,000 of the capital. The expected return doesn't change if we do this. The expected return is 5.2% for each game n, so averaging over 100,000 games still gives us an expected return of 5.2%:

$$E\{r\} = \sum_{n=1}^{N} \left(\frac{1}{N}\right) \cdot E\{r_n\} \Rightarrow 5.2\%. \tag{4.30}$$

The variance of return, however, is quite different. Now we calculate it as follows:

$$Var\{r\} = \sum_{n=1}^{N} \left(\frac{1}{N}\right)^2 \cdot Var\{r_n\} = \left(\frac{Var\{r_n\}}{N}\right) \Rightarrow (0.32\%)^2. \tag{4.31}$$

The casino's expected return is the same in both scenarios. However, the casino clearly much prefers the second scenario from a reward-to-risk ratio standpoint. In the first scenario, the casino has a 47.4% chance of losing $2.5 million. In the second scenario, the casino could lose that much only if it lost 100,000 games in a row, which is enormously unlikely. In fact, Equation 4.31 shows that the standard deviation of casino outcomes is only 0.32%. The casino is unlikely to win more than 5.9% or win less than 4.5%. It has

---

[37]To be more precise, we are analyzing a gamble on evens from the casino's perspective. The casino's signal is +1 for odds. But the expected signal is zero because the gamble could have been on odds, in which case the casino's signal would be –1 (i.e., a bet on evens).

Exhibit 4.10. Comparative Roulette Return Distributions

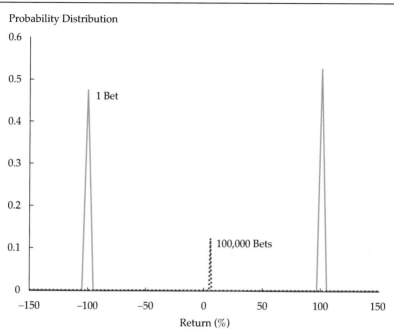

Probability Distribution

effectively locked in winnings of around 5%. **Exhibit 4.10** shows how the return distribution has changed from one scenario to the other.[38]

How does the fundamental law do in this case? We can calculate the information ratio directly and compare it to the fundamental law result with a breadth of 100,000:

$$IR = \frac{5.2\%}{0.32\%} = 16 = IC \cdot \sqrt{BR}. \tag{4.32}$$

In this simple example, breadth works to reduce the variance of outcomes—exactly what we expect from diversification. It doesn't alter the expected return. Its impact on the information ratio is mainly through the denominator.

Understanding the Transfer Coefficient. Now back to the third term in the fundamental law, the transfer coefficient. It measures the correlation between the return of a paper portfolio that optimally implements the manager's views without regard to costs or constraints and the actual portfolio the

---

[38]The graph is a bit misleading because of the very different scales involved in the two distributions. In fact, the area under each distribution is the same: 100%.

manager is running. The information ratio of the paper portfolio is $IC \cdot \sqrt{BR}$. The information ratio of the actual portfolio—taking into account constraints, costs, and possibly even poor implementation—is typically much lower.

To see where the transfer coefficient arises, go back to Equation 4.2, which describes the optimal portfolio, Q:

$$\alpha - 2\lambda \mathbf{V} \cdot \mathbf{h}_Q = 0. \tag{4.33}$$

Portfolio Q is the optimal paper portfolio. Using this relationship, we can calculate the forecast alpha and the information ratio of Portfolio Q:

$$\alpha_Q = \mathbf{h}_Q^T \cdot \alpha \Rightarrow 2\lambda \mathbf{h}_Q^T \cdot \mathbf{V} \cdot \mathbf{h}_Q = 2\lambda \omega_Q^2.$$
$$IR_Q = 2\lambda \omega_Q. \tag{4.34}$$

But the manager holds Portfolio P, not Portfolio Q. We can do a similar calculation, starting again with Equation 4.33:

$$\alpha_P = \mathbf{h}_P^T \cdot \alpha \Rightarrow 2\lambda \mathbf{h}_P^T \cdot \mathbf{V} \cdot \mathbf{h}_Q = 2\lambda \omega_P \cdot \omega_Q \cdot \rho_{PQ}.$$
$$IR_P = 2\lambda \omega_Q \cdot \rho_{PQ} = IR_Q \cdot \rho_{PQ}. \tag{4.35}$$

The information ratio of any Portfolio P is the information ratio of Portfolio Q times the correlation of P and Q. Clarke, de Silva, and Thorley (2002) called that correlation the *transfer coefficient*.

Here are some examples of transfer coefficients to provide insight into its magnitude. Let's assume for these first two examples that residual returns are uncorrelated (the Sharpe 1963 assumption), residual risks are the same for every asset, and scores are normally distributed. If Portfolio P was equal weighted, with long positions for all the positive alpha stocks and short positions for all the negative alpha stocks, it would have a transfer coefficient of $\sqrt{\dfrac{2}{\pi}} \approx 0.8$. Roughly speaking, 80% of our information comes from the sign of the alpha. Further, what if Portfolio P consists of Portfolio Q with, for example, the 25% smallest positions removed? **Exhibit 4.11** shows the general result.

Until you remove about 80% of the smallest positions, the impact on the transfer coefficient is small. Insight 7 will go into much more detail on how the long-only constraint affects the transfer coefficient. For now, I will just note that the transfer coefficient can vary widely across different approaches to investing. At the high end, long–short portfolios of low-transaction-cost

Exhibit 4.11. Transfer Coefficient as We Exclude Small Positions

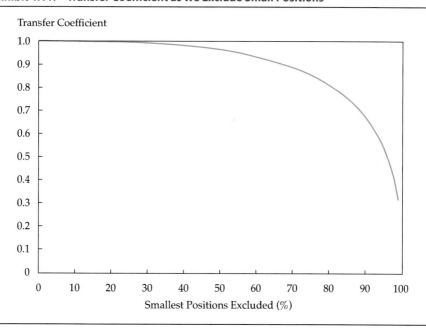

assets (such as futures contracts) can achieve transfer coefficients well above 0.9. But long-only portfolios with additional constraints and high levels of residual risk can experience transfer coefficients well below 0.5.

Investment Examples. Now let's consider four investment examples. First, imagine a stock picker with an information coefficient of 0.05, a small but reasonably impressive level of skill in the active equity management business. This manager follows 500 stocks per quarter, effectively taking 2,000 bets per year. The manager then builds a long-only portfolio with a transfer coefficient of 0.35. The fundamental law implies an information ratio of 0.78 $(0.05 \cdot \sqrt{2,000} \cdot 0.35)$, indicative of a top-quartile manager.

Second, consider a market timer who looks at fundamentals, such as dividend yields and interest rates, and develops skillful new forecasts with an information coefficient of 0.1 roughly once per quarter. This manager runs a long-only portfolio with a transfer coefficient of 0.6. The fundamental law implies an information ratio of 0.12 $(0.1 \cdot \sqrt{4} \cdot 0.6)$, much lower than our stock picker with half the skill in forecasting returns. It is difficult to deliver consistent performance through market timing. It is, of course, possible to deliver significant performance in one quarter through market timing. That is its appeal. But it's hard to repeat that performance quarter after quarter. That

57

is why I stated at the beginning of the chapter that managers focus (or should focus) more on forecasting residual returns than on the market's return.

For the third example, consider the performance of a tactical asset allocation manager who switches between stocks, bonds, and cash. Assume that this manager has a high level of skill for every bet, with an information coefficient of 0.1. This manager looks at broad macroeconomic trends and develops new views about once per quarter, making 12 independent bets per year (quarterly views on the three asset classes). The manager runs a long-only portfolio with a transfer coefficient of 0.5. In this case, the fundamental law implies an information ratio of 0.17, a bit above the median for active managers. Compared with the stock picker, a higher level of skill per bet does not necessarily translate into a higher information ratio. This is a bit better than market timing, owing to slightly more diversification. Because of the influence of the fundamental law of active management, neither market timing nor tactical asset allocation is a popular strategy anymore.

Finally, let's imagine that our tactical asset allocation manager has made these calculations and determined to improve the information ratio by converting the existing fund into a global macro hedge fund. This fund involves similar analysis, which is now applied to asset classes globally and implemented in an unconstrained long–short portfolio. Let's assume the manager expands from forecasting the behavior of three asset classes quarterly to forecasting 25 asset classes quarterly and, in the process, lowers the average information coefficient to 0.08—still respectably high. By going to a long–short structure and by mainly using futures contracts instead of physical investments, the transfer coefficient rises from 0.5 to 0.9. The resulting information ratio rises to 0.72, which is close to the result for the stock-picking strategy.

The fundamental law of active management has several implications. First, successful strategies require some winning combination of skill, breadth, and efficiency. Skill is the hardest to obtain. Breadth (i.e., diversification) can be the easiest to obtain—for example, by following more stocks—but it works only in combination with skill. We can increase efficiency by eliminating constraints. When hiring managers, investors must understand how they combine skill, breadth, and efficiency. This is one way the fundamental law of active management helps investors choose active managers. In the examples, we saw that market timing and tactical asset allocation strategies had trouble putting together compelling combinations of skill, breadth, and efficiency.

Note that, in spite of its mathematical nature, the fundamental law of active management applies to all active managers, not just quantitative managers.

In summary, information ratios, the key to active management, depend on skill, diversification, and efficiency.

Insight 6. Data Mining Is Easy

Why is it that so many strategies look great in backtests and disappoint on implementation? Backtesters always have 95% confidence in their results, so why are investors disappointed far more than 5% of the time? It turns out to be surprisingly easy to search through historical data and find patterns that have no predictive power for the future.

Investment researchers have long used the term *data mining* pejoratively for the unguided search for patterns in historical data. This approach in general is not effective in finding useful signals for predicting asset returns. Over the past decade or so, however, data mining has become a positive term describing research into extremely large datasets, looking for patterns with higher signal-to-noise ratios than typically observed in investing. Today, for example, parents might be delighted to hear that their son wants to marry his data miner girlfriend. Data mining does have a useful and important role in fields with large amounts of data and reasonable signal-to-noise ratios. The larger the amount of data, the lower the required signal-to-noise ratio. Still, investment research often uses data mining as a derogatory term because many of our datasets are not that big and our signal-to-noise ratios are typically low.

To understand why data mining is easy, we must first understand the statistics of coincidence. Let's begin with some non-investment examples and then move on to investment research.

Non-Investment Examples. In the mid-1980s, Evelyn Adams won the New Jersey state lottery twice in four months. Newspapers put the odds of that happening at 17 trillion to 1, an incredibly improbable event. Soon afterward, two Purdue University statisticians, Stephen M. Samuels and George P. McCabe, Jr., showed that a double win in the lottery is not a particularly improbable event.[39] They estimated the odds against observing a double winner in four months at only 30 to 1. What explains the enormous discrepancy in these two probabilities?

It turns out that the odds of Evelyn Adams (specifically her) winning the lottery twice are in fact 17 trillion to 1. But millions of people play the lottery every day. Thus, the odds of *someone*, somewhere, winning two lotteries in four months are only 30 to 1. If it weren't Evelyn Adams, it would have been someone else. In fact, it has happened again since then.

---

[39]Samuels and McCabe (1986), and also Diaconis and Mosteller (1989).

Coincidences appear improbable only when viewed from a narrow perspective. When viewed from the correct (broad) perspective, coincidences are not so improbable. Let's consider another non-investment example: Norman Bloom, arguably the world's greatest data miner.[40]

Bloom died a few years ago in the midst of his quest to prove the existence of God through baseball statistics and the Dow Jones Industrial Average. He argued that "both instruments are in effect great laboratory experiments wherein great amounts of recorded data are collected and published." As but one example of thousands of his analyses of baseball, he argued that it was not a coincidence when the Kansas City Royals' third baseman George Brett hit his third home run in the third game of the playoffs to tie the score 3–3. Rather, it proved the existence of God. In the investment arena, he argued that it was not a coincidence that the Dow's 13 crossings of the 1,000-point line in 1976 mirrored the 13 colonies that united in 1776. He also pointed out that the 12th crossing occurred on his birthday, deftly combining message and messenger. He never took into account the enormous volume of data he searched through—in fact, an entire New York Public Library's worth—to find these coincidences. His focus was narrow, not broad.

The importance of perspective to understanding the statistics of coincidence was perhaps best summarized by, of all people, the novelist Marcel Proust (1982, p. 178)—who often showed keen mathematical intuition:

> The number of pawns on the human chessboard being less than the number of combinations that they are capable of forming, in a theater from which all the people we know and might have expected to find are absent, there turns up one whom we never imagined that we should see again and who appears so opportunely that the coincidence seems to us providential, although, no doubt, some other coincidence would have occurred in its stead had we not been in that place but in some other, where other desires would have been born and another old acquaintance forthcoming to help us satisfy them.

Investment Examples. Investment research involves exactly the same statistics and the same issues of perspective. The typical investment data mining example involves *t*-statistics gathered from backtesting strategies. The narrow perspective says, "After 19 false starts, this 20th investment strategy finally works. It has a *t*-statistic of 2."

But the broad perspective on this situation is quite different. In fact, given 20 informationless strategies, the probability of finding at least 1 with a *t*-statistic of 2 is 64%. The narrow perspective substantially inflates our confidence

---

[40]For more on Norman Bloom, see Sagan (1977).

in the results. When viewed from the proper perspective, confidence in the results falls accordingly.

Given that data mining is easy, how can we safeguard against it? Over time, my team at BlackRock has developed a number of approaches that work effectively for investment research.

To start, one should judge any new investment idea on the basis of whether it is

- sensible,

- predictive,

- consistent, and

- additive.

The sensibility criterion forces us to consider why an idea might work—and, relatedly, why the market doesn't already understand it—before testing it empirically. This criterion allows an empirical analysis to proceed only if we have a reason to believe it might work. Although sensibility may sound overly restrictive in a world of statistical learning and data-driven understanding, three key issues lie behind its use: the amount of data, the signal-to-noise ratio, and non-stationarity. Where we have plenty of data, high signal-to-noise ratios, and stationary processes, we can rely on statistical learning without *ex ante* sensibility. There are even areas of investing where we can relax the sensibility criterion: notably, higher-frequency phenomena, such as short-horizon trading signals. But overall, my team at BlackRock has found sensibility to be effective in leading toward valuable research directions.

The other three criteria concern the backtest results themselves. We obviously seek predictive signals—ideas that predict future returns as opposed to those that contemporaneously help explain returns. Backtests probe a signal's ability to predict returns over historical data. Consistency ties directly to high information ratios. We actually care about the consistency of our aggregate forecast rather than the consistency of any one component signal. The additivity criterion judges whether this is a new idea or an old idea disguised as new. Having been in this business for many years, I can say that sometimes what we think of as new ideas are already contained in the existing aggregate forecast.

Beyond these four criteria, ancillary testing of any new idea also helps in determining its potential effectiveness. Our goal is to understand how the idea affects investment returns and, hence, to develop non-return tests. For example, is this an equity idea that predicts earnings surprise (the difference between newly reported earnings and analyst expected earnings) and influences returns through that mechanism? The ancillary test can check whether the signal predicts earnings surprise. This ancillary test provides a second statistical test of the signal's efficacy, increasing our statistical confidence in the result. Going forward, it can provide an early indication if the signal stops working.

We also use the statistical techniques of out-of-sample testing and cross-validation. Out-of-sample testing requires us to hold out part of our historical data. We test and fit the signal on the in-sample data and then run a final test with the out-of-sample data. The held-out sample might be the most recent historical period, but it could also be a subset of the assets.

Cross-validation breaks the data into N periods and then tests and fits the data N times, each time with one of those periods held out. Both approaches limit overfitting to a particular sample of the data.

What Fraction of Positive Backtest Results Are True? I have attempted to estimate the impact of this overall approach on the ability to successfully identify effective signals, using a methodology proposed by John Ioannidis in his provocative 2005 article on medical research, "Why Most Published Research Results Are False." Ioannidis's analysis is top down. He started by thinking about all the medical studies that have been done and placing each experiment into a 2×2 table (see **Exhibit 4.12**). To fill out the table, imagine a total of c studies. Ioannidis applied a measure of degree of difficulty, R_{pn}, the *ex ante* expected ratio of positive results to negative results. This measure shows, *ex ante*, how many studies are likely to be positive and how many are likely to be negative. Is the research looking for fish in barrels or needles in haystacks? If the researcher is considering 100 different studies and R_{pn} is 1:9, then she expects 10 studies to find a positive result and 90 studies to find a negative result.

Ioannidis then added to his analysis several important considerations:

- f_{fp}, the fraction of false positives caused by statistical noise

- f_{fn}, the fraction of false negatives caused by statistical noise

- b, for bias (Researchers will present some fraction of negative results as positive owing to bias. Statistical noise, bias, or both will lead true negative results to be presented as positive.)

- N, for number of multiple tests (We have discussed this already—testing multiple variants of the signal until we find a variant that works. This increases false positives because the researcher reports a positive result even if only one out of N tests show up positive.)

Exhibit 4.12. Research Findings and True Relationships

True Relationships

	Positive	Negative

Research Findings — Positive / Negative

Source: Ioannidis (2005).

After putting this all together, as shown in Exhibit 4.12, he then looked at the sum of the top row—all the results that have tested positive—and asked what fraction of those results actually are positive? This measure is the *positive predictive value* (PPV), and it depends on all the variables introduced above. (See the Technical Appendix at the end of this chapter for more details.)

Ioannidis (2005) showed that most published medical research has a PPV of less than 50%—hence, the article's title. He also described how research findings are less likely to be true

- the smaller the study;

- the smaller the effect size;

- the greater the flexibility in designs, definitions, and analyses;

- the greater the financial interest; and

- the hotter the field of study.

He stated that "finally, … before running an experiment, investigators should consider what they believe the chances are that they are testing a true rather than a non-true relationship" (p. 701). That sounds a lot like our criterion of sensibility.

Edward L. Glaeser (2008) covered some of the same ground as Ioannidis, though his work focused on economic research and had less analytical structure. He provided more detail, in particular, on researcher bias caused by incentives faced by assistant professors. He cautioned skepticism of methodological complexity, which offers researchers more degrees of freedom and increases the cost of reproducing results. He also called for skepticism toward analysts who produce and clean their own data, another opportunity for increasing statistical significance.

Financial research isn't the same as medical research. We are looking not for truths of nature but, rather, for relationships we hope will work for some period of time. We live in a non-stationary world and expect that most of our investment ideas will eventually stop working as the market discovers them. Still, we can use a variant of Exhibit 4.12, where the columns are not about truth but, rather, are about adding value, or not, out of sample. (The Technical Appendix at the end of this chapter provides more details.)

I have used this analysis to estimate the importance of the research criteria and ancillary testing to boosting the positive predictive value—the fraction of signals that pass the tests and work out of sample. **Exhibit 4.13** shows the results, along with specific values I chose for the key variables.

We start with scattershot data mining—searching for patterns in data without any prior reason to believe they're there (i.e., no *ex ante* sensibility)—and run about 20 tests looking for the best results. The PPV is about 10%. In my estimation, adding sensibility boosts the PPV to just under 50%. The full approach described previously—with the four criteria plus ancillary testing—raises the PPV to 75%. Although many of the inputs to the analysis are just rough estimates, it is clear that this approach significantly affects the PPV.

Exhibit 4.13. Research Environment and Positive Predictive Value

Research Environment	f_{fp}	f_{fn}	Bias	N	R_{pn}	PPV
Scattershot data mining	0.05	0.01	0.1	20	0.1	10%
No SPCA* process	0.05	0.05	0.2	10	0.15	14
Sensibility	0.05	0.05	0.2	3	0.5	47
SPCA, ancillary testing	0.01	0.05	0.05	3	0.5	75

*SPCA stands for sensible, predictive, consistent, and additive.
Source: BlackRock.

Insight 7. Constraints and Costs Have a Surprisingly Large Impact

The final insight is that constraints and costs can have a surprisingly substantial impact. To illustrate this point, I focus on the long-only constraint, one of the most pervasive and impactful constraints. Most investing is long only. Here, I show the impact of that constraint.

Conveniently, we have a tool to measure the impact of constraints and costs: the transfer coefficient. Constraints and costs affect the efficiency of our implementation, so the transfer coefficient quantifies the impact.

Imagine that we follow a universe of stocks and that our views of them are roughly normally distributed. In the language of stock recommendations, some are strong buys, some are strong sells, and the majority are closer to the middle. **Exhibit 4.14** shows the situation schematically.

Intuitively, the long-only constraint limits our ability to fully take advantage of the most negative information—that is, those assets to the left of the blue dotted line in Exhibit 4.14. If that blue line is far to the left, we affect only a few positions. As it moves toward the center, though, it affects more and more assets. What influences the position of that blue line? A key driver is the residual risk of the fund.

Exhibit 4.14. Impact of the Long-Only Constraint

Number of Recommendations

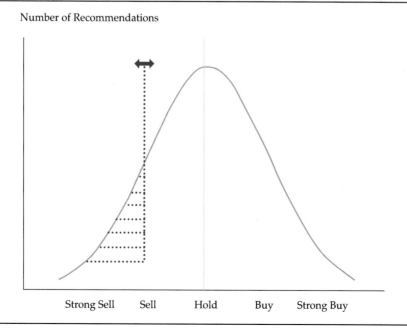

Strong Sell　　Sell　　Hold　　Buy　　Strong Buy

　　65

As we increase the fund's residual risk, we take bigger overweights and bigger underweights. As the underweights increase, they increasingly run into the long-only constraint. We expect the impact of the long-only constraint to increase and the transfer coefficient to decrease as the residual risk of the fund increases.

In fact, the impact of the constraint is bigger than this analysis implies. It also affects assets with positive recommendations, because our overweights and underweights need to balance. We can overweight an asset only if we underweight another asset. If we are limited in our ability to underweight, owing to the long-only constraint, we will hence be limited in our ability to overweight.

Simplified Example. Consider this interesting, yet simple, example. We start with an equal-weighted 1,000-stock benchmark. Each stock has a 0.1% weight in the benchmark. Assume that each stock has the same residual risk, that residual returns are uncorrelated (the Sharpe 1963 assumption), and we generate forecast alphas as $IC \cdot \omega \cdot z$, with IC and ω the same for every stock and z generated from a normal distribution. We calculate optimal holdings for a long–short fund as well as for a long-only fund. **Exhibit 4.15** shows the optimal holdings of the two funds, displayed with the stocks sorted from largest forecast alpha to smallest forecast alpha.

The long–short portfolio holdings look roughly symmetric, with roughly the same amount long and short. The portfolio includes about 500 long positions and 500 short positions. The largest positive positions look similar to the largest negative positions.

The long-only portfolio looks very different. We know the smallest possible position is a 0.1% underweight—that is, a holding of zero in the portfolio—and about 700 stocks have that position. Clearly, the positions of the negative-alpha stocks look quite different for these two portfolios. Exhibit 4.15 also shows the impact of the long-only constraint on positive positions. Just compare optimal holdings in the two portfolios for the largest positive-alpha stocks. These are notably smaller in the long-only portfolio. In fact, the long–short portfolio turns out to be 202% long and 202% short, whereas the long-only portfolio is only 73% overweight and 73% underweight.[41] This exhibit provides graphic evidence that the long-only constraint also affects holdings for the most positive alphas because of the constraint that longs and shorts must balance out.

A More Realistic Analysis. To estimate the impact of the long-only constraint in more realistic portfolios, Grinold and I (2000) used a simulation

---

[41]These numbers were calculated by summing the long positions and the overweights, respectively.

Exhibit 4.15. Long-Only and Long–Short Active Positions

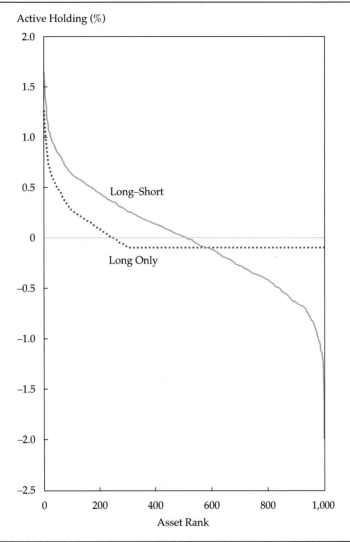

Active Holding (%)

experiment. We started with a benchmark 500-stock portfolio. To use realistic asset weights, we first analyzed several popular cap-weighted equity indexes, including the S&P 500 and the Russell 1000. Although these differ somewhat, their asset weights are not far from lognormally distributed. So, we used a lognormal distribution fit to those typical benchmarks.

With the benchmark set, we generated 900 sets of 500 alpha forecasts. Each set of 500 alphas had an intrinsic information ratio of 1.5. We sampled the alpha forecasts from a distribution uncorrelated with cap-weight. For each set, we built optimal long–short and long-only portfolios of different residual risk levels. We then calculated the forecast alpha and residual risk for each portfolio. After doing that 900 times, we averaged the result for each risk level.

One reason we did multiple simulations is that although the underlying distribution of alphas is uncorrelated with cap-weight, particular samples of alphas might randomly end up correlated with cap-weight. If the alphas were accidentally negatively correlated with cap-weight, such that the larger-cap stocks tended to have more negative alphas, the long-only constraint would be a bit less binding, and vice versa. We generated 900 simulations and then averaged over those accidental correlations, positive and negative. **Exhibit 4.16** displays the resulting efficient frontiers.

The long–short efficient frontier displays an information ratio of 1.5. For example, we have an expected alpha of 6% when our residual risk is 4%, and the efficient frontier is a straight line.

The long-only efficient frontier shows the increasing impact of the constraint with increasing residual risk. It is true that as we increase residual risk, we increase forecast alpha. However, we receive less and less additional forecast alpha for each additional unit of residual risk.

Exhibit 4.16. Efficient Frontier

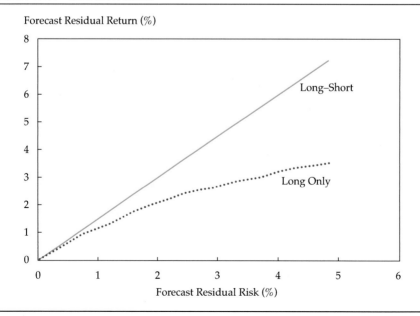

Forecast Residual Return (%)

Forecast Residual Risk (%)

Exhibit 4.17. Transfer Coefficient

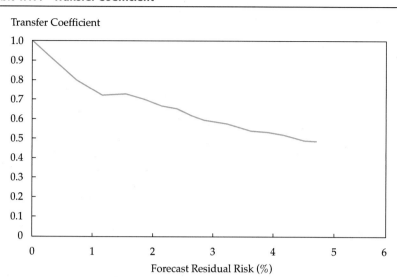

We can also see this effect by looking directly at the transfer coefficient as a function of residual risk, as in **Exhibit 4.17**.

The transfer coefficient for each risk level is simply the ratio of the long-only information ratio to the long–short information ratio. The higher the residual risk, the lower the transfer coefficient.

According to this fairly realistic simulation study, at 2% residual risk, the long-only constraint reduces the information ratio by about 30%, and at 4.5% residual risk, typical for US active equity mutual funds,[42] the long-only constraint reduces the information ratio by about 50%.

Beyond the loss in information ratio, the long-only constraint also induces a small size bias that increases with residual risk. We are more constrained in underweighting small stocks than large stocks in cap-weighted benchmarks. We can start with forecast alphas uncorrelated with size and build a long-only portfolio with a bet on small stocks outperforming large stocks.

Constraints and costs—and the long-only constraint, in particular—can significantly affect expected performance. We are better off running long-only portfolios at low residual risk and using long–short implementations if we wish to run higher-residual-risk portfolios.

---

[42]In the Chapter 5 section on fee compression, I discuss data showing that median active risk levels for US large-cap mutual funds was 4.79% over the period from October 1997 through September 2017.

Summary

These seven insights into active management, viewed broadly, show that active management isn't easy and that the majority of attempts will fail. The information ratio is the critical statistic for investors and active managers. Successful investors must find winning combinations of skill, breadth, and efficiency.

Technical Appendix

This appendix provides more-detailed analysis to estimate positive predictive value.

We start by assuming we test c signals. The number c will drop out of the analysis at the end, but it's clarifying to keep it in for now. The variable R_{pn} measures the *ex ante* ratio of positive results to negative results. It measures the degree of difficulty of our research. We, therefore, expect that $\dfrac{c \cdot R_{pn}}{R_{pn}+1}$ are truly positive and $\dfrac{c}{R_{pn}+1}$ are truly negative. Of the results that are truly negative, f_{fp} of them will test positive and $(1-f_{fp})$ of them will test negative. We can similarly analyze what happens to the truly positive results, which lead to **Exhibit 4A.1**.

We can see from Exhibit 4A.1 that the positive predictive value is

$$PPV = \frac{R_{pn} \cdot (1 - f_{fn})}{R_{pn} \cdot (1 - f_{fn}) + f_{fp}}. \tag{4.36}$$

As the *ex ante* probability increases and the false positives and negatives decrease, it can approach 1. Of course, it can also fall far below 1.

It turns out that the *ex ante* ratio of positive results to negative results can have a big impact on the positive predictive value. To see why that happens, imagine that your doctor tests you for a rare disease; only 1 person out of 1,000 has this disease. The test is 99% accurate—that is, the fraction of false positives is 1%—and assume there are no false negatives. The test comes back positive. How likely is it that you have the disease? The answer is not 99% but only about 1 out of 11. Equation 4.36 also leads to that answer.

What's going on here? Out of 1,000 people, 1 is a true positive and 999 are true negatives. If we apply the 1% false positive rate to the 999 true negatives, we expect to see about 10 false positives. The group of people who will test positive includes 1 true positive and 10 false positives. The probability of having the disease after testing positive is about 1 out of 11.

We can now see why the *ex ante* ratio of positive results to negative results can significantly affect our results. If we are testing many signals with low

Exhibit 4A.1. Research Findings and True Relationships

True Relationships

	Positive	Negative
Positive	$c \cdot \left(\dfrac{R_{pn}}{R_{pn}+1} \right) \cdot (1 - f_{fn})$	$c \cdot \left(\dfrac{1}{R_{pn}+1} \right) \cdot f_{fp}$
Negative	$c \cdot \left(\dfrac{R_{pn}}{R_{pn}+1} \right) \cdot f_{fn}$	$c \cdot \left(\dfrac{1}{R_{pn}+1} \right) \cdot (1 - f_{fp})$

Research Findings (row label)

$$\text{Total True} = c \cdot \left(\frac{R_{pn}}{R_{pn}+1} \right) \qquad \text{Total False} = c \cdot \left(\frac{1}{R_{pn}+1} \right)$$

Source: Ioannidis (2005).

probabilities of being true, all those truly negative signals can generate many false positives and even swamp the numbers of truly positive signals.

We can also embellish the prior analysis to include two additional effects: bias and multiple testing. For bias, let b represent the fraction of truly negative signals presented as positive owing to bias. In the details of the analysis, assume that truly negative results are presented as negative in the absence of bias and statistical noise. In other words, statistical noise, bias, or both will lead to negative results reported as positive.

As for multiple tests, they increase the probability of false positives. Whereas before f_{fp} measured the fraction of false positives, now $1 - (1 - f_{fp})^N$ measures this fraction. If $N = 1$, the outcome is the same as our prior result, but the probability of false positives increases with each additional set of tests.

Putting this all together, we have **Exhibit 4A.2**.

We also update our formula for positive predictive value to account for these embellishments:

Exhibit 4A.2. Research Findings and True Relationships

Research Findings	True Relationships: Positive	True Relationships: Negative
Positive	$c\cdot\left(\frac{R_{pn}}{R_{pn}+1}\right)\cdot\left\{1-\left[(1-b)\cdot f_{fn}\right]^N\right\}$	$c\cdot\left(\frac{1}{R_{pn}+1}\right)\cdot\left\{1-\left[(1-b)\cdot(1-f_{fp})\right]^N\right\}$
Negative	$c\cdot\left(\frac{R_{pn}}{R_{pn}+1}\right)\cdot\left[(1-b)\cdot f_{fn}\right]^N$	$c\cdot\left(\frac{1}{R_{pn}+1}\right)\cdot\left[(1-b)\cdot(1-f_{fp})\right]^N$
	Total True $= c\cdot\left(\frac{R_{pn}}{R_{pn}+1}\right)$	Total False $= c\cdot\left(\frac{1}{R_{pn}+1}\right)$

Sources: Ioannidis (2005), BlackRock, and author.

$$PPV=\frac{R_{pn}\cdot\left\{1-\left[(1-b)\cdot f_{fn}\right]^N\right\}}{R_{pn}\cdot\left\{1-\left[(1-b)\cdot f_{fn}\right]^N\right\}+1-\left[(1-b)\cdot(1-f_{fp})\right]^N}. \tag{4.37}$$

Note that if we set $b=0$ and $N=1$, we end up with Equation 4.36.

Bibliography

Clarke, Roger, Harindra de Silva, and Steven Thorley. 2002. "Portfolio Constraints and the Fundamental Law of Active Management." *Financial Analysts Journal* (September/October): 48–66.

Diaconis, Persi, and Frederick Mosteller. 1989. "Methods for Studying Coincidences." *Journal of the American Statistical Association* 84 (408, Applications and Case Studies): 853–61.

Fama, Eugene F., and Kenneth R. French. 2010. "Luck versus Skill in the Cross-Section of Mutual Fund Returns." *Journal of Finance* 65 (5): 1915–47.

Glaeser, Edward L. 2008. "Researcher Incentives and Empirical Methods." In *The Foundations of Positive and Normative Economics: A Hand Book*, edited by Andrew Caplin and Andrew Schotter. Oxford, UK: Oxford University Press.

Grinold, Richard C. 1989. "The Fundamental Law of Active Management." *Journal of Portfolio Management* 15 (3): 30–37.

Grinold, Richard C., and Ronald N. Kahn. 2000. *Active Portfolio Management*, 2nd ed. New York: McGraw-Hill.

Grinold, Richard C., and Ronald N. Kahn. 2000. "The Efficiency Gains of Long-Short Investing." *Financial Analysts Journal* 56 (6): 40–53.

Grinold, Richard C., and Ronald N. Kahn. 2011. "Breadth, Skill, and Time." *Journal of Portfolio Management* (Fall): 18–28.

Ioannidis, John P. A. 2005. "Why Most Published Research Findings Are False." *PLoS Medicine* 2 (8): 696–701.

Kahn, Ronald N. 1999. "Seven Quantitative Insights into Active Management." *Barra Newsletter* from Barra and *Investment Insights* from Barclays Global Investors.

Proust, Marcel. 1982. *Remembrance of Things Past: The Guermantes Way, Cities of the Plain*, Vol. 2. New York: Vintage Books.

Sagan, Carl. 1977. "God and Norman Bloom." *American Scholar* 46 (4): 460–6.

Samuels, Stephen M., and George P. McCabe, Jr. 1986. "More Lottery Repeaters Are on the Way." *New York Times*, letter to the editor (17 February).

Sharpe, William F. 1963. "A Simplified Model for Portfolio Analysis." *Management Science* 9 (2): 277–93.

Sharpe, William F. 1991. "The Arithmetic of Active Management." *Financial Analysts Journal* 47 (1): 7–9.

Sharpe, William F. 1992. "Asset Allocation: Management Style and Performance Measurement." *Journal of Portfolio Management* 18 (2): 7–19.

5. Seven Trends in Investment Management

The trends that are shaping the 21st Century embody both promise and peril.

—Klaus Schwab

Now that we have covered the modern history of investment management and have reviewed several insights about active management, we can look forward to where investment management is heading. This chapter covers seven key trends that help forecast the future of investment management over the next 5–10 years:

- Active to passive

- Increased competition

- Changing market environments

- Big data

- Smart beta

- Investing beyond returns

- Fee compression

As I discuss these trends, I make sure to consider whether I expect them to continue. In some cases, the future of investment management will depend on whether a trend continues.

Trend 1. Active to Passive

As previously discussed, the first index fund launched in 1971, after developments in academic finance surprisingly supported the concept of passive investing. Both the capital asset pricing model and the efficient market hypothesis argued that active management was futile and that indexing was the optimal approach to investing.

In the decades after those developments, however, subsequent work identified a number of reasons to believe that successful active management is possible. I have already discussed behavioral finance, excess volatility, arbitrage pricing theory, and informational inefficiency. These four developments provide arguments in favor of active management. Speaking personally, my group at BlackRock—the Systematic Active Equity team—has a record of success in active management that has lasted for more than 30 years. For the first 20 years, we depended significantly on risk premiums and the arbitrage pricing theory, à la Ross (1976). Since then, we have mainly relied on informational inefficiency, à la Grossman–Stiglitz (1980)—processing publicly available information faster than the market.

There are at least two additional reasons to believe in active management, beyond these four arguments. First, most investors face constraints in their investments. Perhaps they can only, or almost only, invest long-only. Perhaps they can invest only in certain regions or markets. Constraints—as we have seen—can significantly affect investor portfolios and limit market efficiency. Second, sometimes large investors find themselves in trouble, needing to raise significant capital quickly. This condition often arises when investors combine leverage with illiquid assets—for example, when Long-Term Capital Management collapsed in 1998. Situations like that, which will continue to occur but at uncertain intervals, provide opportunities for investors with the available liquidity to take advantage of them. These opportunistic investments can enhance active returns but arise only sporadically. They can't be the primary strategy for an active manager.

Where are we now in the debate between active and index investing? **Exhibit 5.1** shows cumulative flows in US equity mutual funds and exchange-traded funds from 2008 through 2017.

Exhibit 5.1. US Domestic Equity Flows ($ billions)

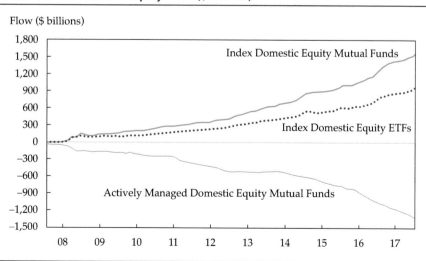

Source: Investment Company Institute (2018).

Exhibit 5.2. Global Exchange-Traded Product Assets, 2000–March 2018

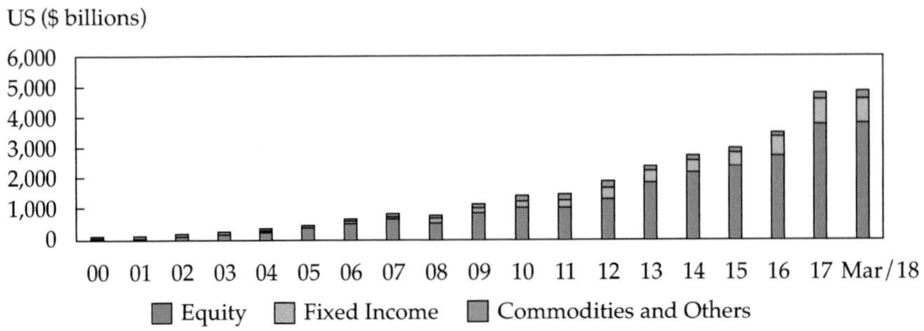

US ($ billions)

Source: BlackRock Global ETP Landscape, Monthly Snapshot (March 2018).

For the past 10 years, we have seen steady flows out of active equity funds and into equity index mutual funds and index ETFs. More than 50 years after the development of the capital asset pricing model, index funds have been gathering substantial assets, at the expense of active funds. Based on fund flows, investors appear to now be heeding the arguments in favor of indexing.

For some perspective, BlackRock estimated that as of year-end 2016, actively managed assets totaled $55.8 trillion and indexed assets totaled $14.4 trillion (in addition, $6.3 trillion was in cash).[43] Even after a decade of shifting out of active equity and into index equity, 79% of assets were still actively managed. The fraction of equity assets that are actively managed is lower than the fraction of fixed-income assets that are actively managed. Ignoring ETFs, multi-asset products, and alternative investments, 72% of equity investments were actively managed and 82% of fixed-income assets were actively managed as of year-end 2016.

Exhibit 5.1 also testifies to a related trend—the enormous growth of the ETF market. **Exhibit 5.2** provides further evidence for how much the ETF market has grown since 2000. As of March 2018, the global ETF market has grown to $4.8 trillion.

The vast majority of ETFs are products that track third-party indexes—that is, indexes developed by a party independent of the investment manager—although many such indexes are not broad market indexes. These products have some advantages over other fund structures. They offer continuous pricing and liquidity—investors can trade them throughout the day—and they are more tax efficient than other fund structures.

---

[43]BlackRock, "Global Industry Heat Map, Q4 2017," p. 2.

To help us understand these flows from active to index, we can look at the track record of active management—a regular topic of academic study. We have discussed arguments for indexing and arguments for why successful active management might be possible. How have these played out over time?

In one often-cited study, Eugene Fama and Kenneth French (2010) examined the performance of US equity mutual funds. I discussed this study in Chapter 4, in the section on the arithmetic of active management. As we will see, US equity mutual funds are often studied by academics, in part owing to their long history and survivorship-bias-free database. Fama and French showed that the average active manager underperformed by roughly the average level of fees. To be specific, within the world of US equity mutual funds, active managers have delivered roughly zero alpha on average before fees over the 33-year period from 1984 through 2006. Their average alpha after fees ranged from –81 bps per year to –113 bps per year, depending on whether Fama and French controlled for one, three, or four factors.[44] Those econometric details don't change the headline result. In a somewhat related result, French (2008) additionally argued that US investors paid 67 bps in aggregate for active management over the same period. That number appears lower than the Fama–French (2010) result, but French measured it across all investments—active and index—so we should expect a lower number.

As we know from the arithmetic of active management, we *expect* the average active manager to underperform. The Fama–French (2010) result seems a bit better than expected, because the average active manager underperformed only by average fees, not by average fees and trading costs. In any event, though, the underperformance of the average active manager says little about whether successful active management is possible.

To focus on that question, we need to look at persistence of performance. Do winners repeat? Even if the average active manager underperforms, persistence of positive active returns year after year would provide evidence that successful active management is possible.

There have been many academic studies of this question over a long period of time. Joop Huij and Simon Lansdorp (2012) wrote one of the more recent papers, and its bibliography includes many of the others.[45] These studies vary

---

[44]Controlling for one factor involves simply regressing fund returns against market returns and examining the intercept (alpha). To control for three factors, Fama and French (2010) added their small size (SMB) and value (HML) factors, as described in Fama and French (1992). To control for four factors, they added Mark Carhart's (1997) momentum factor.

[45]Their paper is on the Social Science Research Network (ssrn.com), though not in a journal yet. Academics post new papers on ssrn.com well before they are accepted and appear in journals. This network has dramatically increased the speed of dissemination of new ideas. An SSRN app, for easily accessing new papers from smartphones, even exists.

by asset class, time period, and methodology—for example, whether they control for fund style and how they do so.

Several of these studies show some evidence for persistence. This evidence ranges from fairly weak in US equity mutual funds to fairly strong in private equity.[46] Regarding the evidence for persistence of performance in US equity mutual funds, here is one simple question: If a mutual fund has above-median performance in one period—such that it is in the top 50% of funds on the basis of performance—what is the probability that it will have above-median performance in the next period? If that probability is 50%, then active performance is as random as a coin toss. I've met many investors who assume that the answer isn't 100%—that persistence isn't perfect—but that maybe it's only 75%. In fact, these studies on US equity mutual funds find probabilities between 50% and 60% and discuss whether those numbers are statistically significant.[47] The data strongly support the standard warning that "past performance is no guarantee of future results."

We can understand the trend of active to passive investing in part because of the historical track record for active management. The average active manager underperforms. There is some evidence for persistence of performance and, hence, some evidence that successful active management is possible. But the evidence in favor of active management isn't overwhelming. We are not sure how much longer the trend from active to passive will continue, but at a minimum, indexing is here to stay as a significant component of investment management.

Trend 2. Increased Competition

Has active management become more competitive? Laurent Barras, Olivier Scaillet, and Russ Wermers (2010) examined US equity mutual funds over the 32-year period from 1975 through 2006. They classified each fund into one of three categories:

- Zero alpha: managers who have skill but only enough to cover their fees

- Skilled: managers who deliver positive alpha to clients after fees and costs

- Unskilled

By their estimate, roughly three-quarters of all managers are zero alpha. Note that they took uncertainty into account when classifying managers into

---

[46]See Steve Kaplan and Antoinette Schoar (2005) for the private equity analysis.
[47]For example, see Kahn and Rudd (1995).

these three categories. These managers don't deliver *exactly* zero alpha after fees, but their alpha is statistically indistinguishable from zero after fees.[48]

Even more interesting is that Barras et al. (2010) estimated that the fraction of skillful active managers has declined from about 15% at the beginning of their sample period to only about 1% at the end of the period. These exact numbers depend on their particular analysis. Without completely and uncritically accepting their exact results, they do seem to show that successful active management has become more difficult. Stated differently, active management has become more competitive over time.

Let's look at this phenomenon from another angle. As I showed in Chapter 3, for instance, in the story told by Victor Niederhoffer, academic finance effectively experienced a long ban on work in support of active management. That ban lasted from the development of the efficient market hypothesis through the eventual academic acceptance of behavioral finance. As behavioral finance established itself, academics started investigating and discovering market inefficiencies. What happens to those inefficiencies after academics publish papers describing them to the world?

In an interesting paper, David McLean and Jeffrey Pontiff (2016) examined the performance of a large set of active investment ideas—that is, market inefficiencies—in three periods: the period used in the published academic study, an out-of-sample period (from the end of the study period to the publication date), and the post-publication period, when the results were available to all. Not surprisingly, much of the active performance disappeared after publication, perhaps in part because some of the ideas were just statistical flukes.

However, McLean and Pontiff (2016) attributed about one-third of the decline in performance to "publication-informed trading." To me, as an active manager myself, this finding isn't surprising. Not only are these academic papers easily available on the Social Science Research Network, but research groups at broker/dealers send out monthly emails listing the new academic papers of most interest to active managers. Speaking as a manager focused on processing publicly available information faster than the market, my team's next great idea is not going to come from SSRN.

At a more anecdotal level, my group at BlackRock has seen the same decline described by McLean and Pontiff (2016). We test new ideas by building a long–short *characteristic* portfolio every period. The characteristic

---

[48]Barras et al. (2010) did take into account the multiple test environment: the fact that even if 1,000 funds had truly zero alpha after fees, 50 of them (5%) would appear to deliver significant alpha owing to random fluctuations—positive or negative—at the 95% confidence level, if interpreted as 1,000 separate single tests.

portfolio is long stocks with positive exposure to the idea and short stocks with negative exposure, while minimizing all other risks. The performance of the characteristic portfolio should be driven by the underlying idea, since we have minimized all other exposures and risks.

Exhibit 5.3 shows the performance of three particular academic ideas displayed as event studies, with $t = 0$ defined as the publication date. The first two ideas concern quality of earnings, with one published in 1996 and the other in 2001. The third idea, which appeared in 2008, uses information from option markets to forecast stock returns. The first idea worked more often than not for at least five years after publication. The second idea worked for about two years after publication. The third idea never worked after publication. These are just anecdotal observations—we can't extrapolate too much on the basis of just three observations—but they are consistent with McLean and Pontiff (2016). We discussed these observations with clients before the McLean and Pontiff article appeared.

The changing regulatory environment has also increased competitiveness by eliminating advantages of large investors over small investors. One key development here was Regulation Fair Disclosure, or Reg FD, issued by the US Securities and Exchange Commission in August 2000. This rule required

Exhibit 5.3. Idea Performance before and after Publication

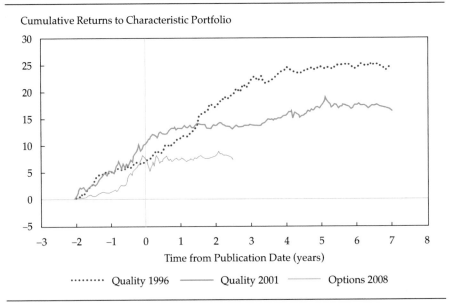

Cumulative Returns to Characteristic Portfolio

Source: BlackRock.

all publicly traded companies to release all material nonpublic information to all investors at the same time. Previously, such information was selectively released to large institutions first. For example, most companies did not invite small investors to their quarterly earnings conference calls, possibly in part because of technological challenges. The development of the internet and webcasting tools helped facilitate broad access.

One result of Reg FD was that institutional investor meetings with company management became less informative. Companies are not allowed to selectively disclose any material information. It is possible that investors can learn valuable information in such meetings via body language or other subtle and unintended clues, but a primary source of information for some investors became less clear or reliable. The competitive edge held by large institutions shrank. In the years since Reg FD, other regulatory efforts have aimed to further erase competitive informational advantages held by large institutions, such as access to information from experts and analysts who follow industries and companies.

As with the first trend, we aren't sure whether active management can become even more competitive than it is today. We do expect it to remain highly competitive.

Trend 3. Changing Market Environments

When I discussed the trend from active to index investing, I portrayed it as a negative for active management. However, there is another side to this. From the perspective of an active manager, the other side of any trade is increasingly likely to be an *uninformed* index fund—that is, a trader with no specific knowledge or insight about the particular asset being traded. This fact potentially improves the opportunities for active managers: They are more likely to be trading with uninformed investors.

That said, the overall trading environment has changed in many ways over the past 20 years. **Exhibit 5.4** shows trends in the average trade size (from the consolidated tape of all trades of stocks listed on the NYSE) on the right-hand axis and NYSE block share volume as a percentage of consolidated share volume on the left-hand axis.

Exhibit 5.4 clearly shows that today's trading environment is very different from what it was in 2004. This exhibit shows the emergence of high-frequency trading. In principle, the other side of an active manager's trade is more likely than ever to be an index fund. However, the intermediary facilitating that trade is now a high-frequency trader.

The average trade size has declined from about 1,000 shares per trade to about 200 shares per trade. Traders are breaking up large trades into multiple

Exhibit 5.4. The Changing Trading Environment

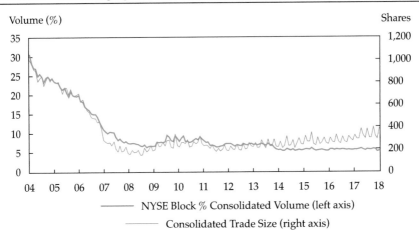

Note: Data cover stocks listed on the NYSE.
Sources: NYSE and BlackRock.

small trades. Consistent with this trend, block volume was about 30% of total volume in 2004 but only 10% in 2018. The 10% figure is a bit misleading, however, because we are tracking NYSE block volume over consolidated volume. The NYSE's volume has decreased from about 80% of consolidated volume to only about 20% over this period, but NYSE volume still dominates the opening and closing auction volumes that are included in the block trade numbers. Given the increasing popularity of market-on-close orders—especially from index-tracking funds—a ballpark estimate of current block share volume as a percentage of total share volume is about 15%–18%, still much lower than in 2004.[49]

To summarize, Exhibit 5.4 shows that broker/dealers, who used to be the main source of liquidity, have been replaced by high-frequency traders providing liquidity. The broker/dealers facilitated block trading, and they are decreasingly prevalent. To try to limit the price impact of trading with high-frequency traders, investors are breaking up large trades into smaller ones, in part to try to appear to be uninformed small investors.

The trading environment is very different from what it was 20 years ago. I'm not predicting it will change even further, just noting that investors need to adapt to what has already happened.

---

[49]Thanks to Hubert De Jesus, global head of market structure and electronic trading at BlackRock, for compiling and analyzing these data.

Trend 4. Big Data

So far, I have mainly discussed negative trends for active management. However, this fourth trend—the explosion of available data, also known as *big data*—is definitely positive. In 1985, my group launched its first fund, a US equity fund that attempted to outperform the S&P 500 by overweighting value stocks, momentum stocks, and small stocks. We measured these using, respectively, book-to-price ratios, returns over the prior year, and market capitalization. Our fund's sources of alpha were broadly in line with the arbitrage pricing theory of Stephen Ross (1976). In 1985, our edge was being able to access and process book-to-price ratios for every stock in the S&P 500 and then to optimally blend expected returns based on those characteristics while controlling risk. Few investment firms at that time had all those capabilities. Today, standard financial data are available to everyone with an internet connection—billions of people—although, of course, successfully investing by using those data still requires training and skill.

Beyond financial data, we have seen an explosion in data availability so vast that access is no longer sufficient: The edge now lies in identifying which data are useful and in analyzing and effectively processing them. We commonly refer to this data explosion as "big data." The big data explosion has received a huge amount of press coverage over the past decade. The following are a few magazine cover stories on the topic:

- *Nature:* "Big Data: Science in the Petabyte Era," September 2008

- *The Economist:* "The Data Deluge," 27 February 2010

- *Science:* "Dealing with Data," 11 February 2011

- *Harvard Business Review:* "Getting Control of Big Data," October 2012

- *Foreign Affairs:* "The Rise of Big Data," May/June 2013

- *Der Spiegel:* "Living by the Numbers: Big Data Knows What Your Future Holds," 18 May 2013

- *The Economist:* "The World's Most Valuable Resource: Data and the New Rules of Competition," 6 May 2017

This list doesn't even include technology magazines. Big data is a big mainstream story, and it has been for 10 years.

What does the term "big data" mean? First, it means different things to different people. Google's definition of big data is probably orders of magnitude greater than that of even the most data-focused investment firms. Second, and perhaps most important from our perspective, the data of big data are *unstructured*. Financial reporting data are very structured; we consume them in highly structured datasets provided by Standard & Poor's Compustat, Thompson Reuters Worldscope, and other vendors. For example, Item 36 in the Compustat annual industrial database refers to "retained earnings." The point is that traditionally we could think of fundamental data as existing in a large spreadsheet. Big data not only require much bigger spreadsheets but also don't easily fit into a spreadsheet structure.

Imagine, for example, looking at the text of analyst reports on individual stocks. One common statistic for machine analysis of text is the frequency of usage of particular words and phrases. How often does the word "Microsoft" appear in analyst reports? The answer is pretty often in reports on Microsoft, somewhat often in analyst reports on other technology companies, and not at all often in reports on other companies. If we put together a spreadsheet with a row for each analyst report and columns for various features, the column labeled "Microsoft" would consist mainly of zeros. The spreadsheet would also need an incredibly large number of columns to handle all potentially interesting names and phrases. Both characteristics make unstructured data awkward to store in a spreadsheet structure.

What types of big data potentially provide useful information for active management? Let's examine five general categories: text, search, social media, images, and video.

For a profession that has often focused particularly on numbers, much more of the daily inflow arrives in the form of text. Analysts write reports on individual stocks and describe their business, including its strengths and weaknesses, competitors, potential threats, and the outlook for the future. They also forecast earnings and provide a recommendation, from "strong buy" to "strong sell." Fundamental investors can read through entire reports and consider the implications for stocks they own or are considering purchasing. Quantitative investors, such as my team, who look to analyze every stock in their investment universe in the interest of breadth, have traditionally been able to use only analyst information that arrives in the form of numbers—the earnings forecasts and the recommendations, which were easy to convert to a numerical scale. We ignored most of the document. Now, we can process and interpret the entire analyst report and, for example, understand more about the analyst's sentiment, as well as the nuances around the earnings forecast.

Analyst reports are unstructured in that each analyst writes his own view of a company without trying to fit into any industry-wide template. As a further complication, analyst reports include legal disclaimers. Although these are easy for humans to identify, they represent a bigger challenge for computers. Sometimes they appear at the beginning of a document, sometimes at the end, and sometimes somewhere in between. For sentiment analysis, it's important to distinguish the disclaimer because its sentiment is consistently negative, independent of the analyst's view of the stock.

As of today, an MBA student would do a better job than a computer would do at understanding any one particular analyst report. The computer's edge, though, is in reading the roughly 5,000 analyst reports generated globally every day and analyzing them consistently. And in a few years, computers will beat the MBA student at understanding even a single analyst report. Text analysis, or natural language processing, is a very active research area in computer science. Big data in the form of unstructured text is already a significant input for many quantitative investors.

There are some obvious challenges with text analysis. Text can appear in many different languages. Ultimately, we need to be able to analyze text across those languages. Text can also be ambiguous, especially to a computer. Natural language processing research is working to handle these various challenges.

The second big data category of interest to investors is internet search activity. As the internet has become increasingly ubiquitous, people have come to search for information about everything. For example, Google, with mixed success, has used geo-tagged searches about flu symptoms and remedies to monitor in real time the severity of the flu season.[50] For investors, one example of interesting search activity relates to people researching online before making large purchases of items such as cars and refrigerators. Thus, internet search activity can help us predict sales. Investors have long been predicting future sales, so monitoring internet search activity provides us with new data to improve that effort.

The third big data category of interest to investors is social media: Twitter, Facebook, LinkedIn, and so forth. Social media are varied, as are the potential uses of social media data. Such websites as LinkedIn include data on who works for which companies, who is leaving, and who are the new hires. We can estimate employee sentiment by employee movements. We can estimate whether labor costs are increasing or decreasing on the basis of the number, level, and quality of the new hires and departures. Once again, employee sentiment and labor costs are of long-standing interest to investors. Social media simply represent new sources of data to help predict those quantities.

The fourth and fifth categories are images and video. Investors currently make less use of these categories than the other three, but this will change over the next few years, especially as an increasingly large fraction of all data

---

[50]Ginsberg, Mohebbi, Patel, Brammer, Smolinski, and Brilliant (2009); Butler (2013).

will be image and video data. Fundamental investors currently try to judge body language in in-person meetings with senior management. (This is an important activity in the post-Reg FD era.) Computers can analyze videos of senior management presentations for the same purpose and will be able to analyze all such presentations across the entire investment universe.

Big data represents a huge positive trend for active management, particularly for active managers who embrace the opportunities presented by this development. A closely related advancement, machine learning/artificial intelligence, provides the tools to fully access and analyze this large amount of unstructured data. To gain the benefits of this trend, active managers will need to hire people with skills in these areas—computer scientists, statisticians, data scientists, and applied mathematicians. These people are different from those active managers have typically hired, and they bring different skills.

We are still in the early stages of this trend, in spite of 10 years of magazine cover stories. Increasing amounts of data are becoming available every month, and computer scientists are actively advancing new technologies to analyze these data. A Google search will identify many articles that describe the recent explosive growth in data and that forecast even more growth. To provide specific evidence of this general trend, consider two examples involving demand growth. First, a 2017 report from Burning Glass, IBM, and the Business-Higher Education Forum noted that there were 2,350,000 data science and analytics job openings posted in 2015, forecasted to grow 15% by 2020. The authors expect demand for data scientists and data engineers to grow even faster, by 39%.

As a second example, consider the growth in attendance at the annual Neural Information Processing Systems conference, which is now the world's largest artificial intelligence/machine learning conference. After starting in 1987 with 600 attendees, attendance in recent years has grown from about 1,200 in 2010 to 2,000 in 2013, 5,500 in 2016, and 8,000 in 2017. Industry sponsorship of the conference—a measure of industry interest in research in this area and interest in recruiting people working in this field—grew from 64 sponsors donating $840,000 in 2016 to 84 sponsors donating $1,760,000 in 2017. Demand and interest in big data and machine learning appear poised to continue to grow for the foreseeable future.

Trend 5. Smart Beta

The next trend in investing is *smart beta* or factor investing. Smart beta products are active products with some of the benefits of index products. They are active in that the goal is to outperform the market. They are transparent and rule based, like indexing, with fees between those of active and index products. The nomenclature is not yet set in stone, but currently "smart beta" usually refers to long-only products based on third-party indexes, whereas "factor investing" usually refers to long–short products or long-only products not based on third-party indexes.

Smart beta/factor products provide exposures to broad and persistent factors that have long been a part of active management. For equities, these include small size, value, momentum, quality, and low volatility. For fixed income, the factors include duration and credit. These factors have generated investor interest because they have performed well historically. Beyond that, there are reasons to believe they will continue to outperform in the future. Some of these factors are risk factors, which have associated expected risk premiums. Small size, value, duration, and credit fall into this category. Some of these factors exploit behavioral anomalies and have positive expected returns for that reason. Momentum and quality, and possibly also value, are examples. Finally, some of these factors exploit structural impediments, such as typical investor constraints. The typical constraint on leverage seems to underlie the performance of the low-volatility factor. Seeking high returns without using leverage, investors choose high-volatility stocks and overpay for them.

Factor investing is not new. It goes right back to the arbitrage pricing theory proposed by Stephen Ross in 1976. The ideas underlying these factors go back even further. Value investing, for example, goes back at least to Graham and Dodd in the 1930s and the Dutch investment trusts of the late 1700s, if not even further.

Smart beta/factor products have been rapidly growing over the past several years. According to Jennifer Thompson (2017) of the *Financial Times*, smart beta funds surpassed $1 trillion in assets as of mid-December 2017.

Smart beta/factor products are not without controversy. They are disrupting active management and threaten indexing, with their promise of extra return while retaining the low cost and transparency of indexing. Referring to an early smart beta product, which predated the term "smart beta," John Bogle, the founder of Vanguard and a leading proponent of broad market indexing, said that "fundamental indexing is witchcraft" in an interview with Christine Benz of Morningstar in 2008.

Smart beta/factor investing is more than just a new product; it is a disruptive innovation for active management, as described in Kahn and Lemmon (2016). It's odd to call it an innovation at all. As we have seen, these ideas have been around for decades. But it isn't an investment innovation, it's a *product* innovation. Smart beta/factor investing takes important components of successful active management, carves them out, and sells them for fees below active fees. That's the disruptive innovation.

These smart beta factors are already part of investment management. **Exhibit 5.5** shows a decomposition of investment returns.

We first decompose investment returns into the cap-weighted index benchmark return and the active return.[51] This decomposition requires nothing more than subtraction. The active return is simply the total investment return minus the benchmark return:

$$\delta_p(t) \equiv r_p(t) - r_B(t). \tag{5.1}$$

This decomposition is standard and easy to do.

The next level of decomposition requires just a bit more work. I decompose the active return into two pieces:

- Active return due to static exposures to smart beta factors
- *Pure alpha* return

Exhibit 5.5.   Decomposition of Investment Returns

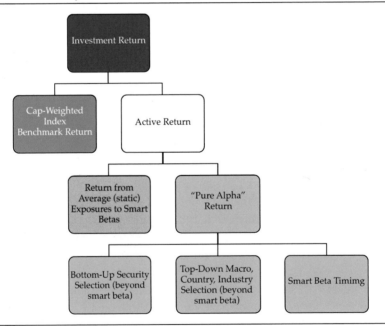

---

[51]For simplicity, here I focus on long-only investment products. The analysis applies equally well to long–short investing, although in that case the benchmark is typically cash rather than a cap-weighted index.

This decomposition requires a time-series regression of active returns against returns to J smart beta factors:

$$\delta_p(t) = \sum_{j=1}^{J} \beta_j \cdot b_j(t) + u_p(t). \tag{5.2}$$

For an equity strategy, one might use the five standard smart beta factors: small size, value, momentum, quality, and low volatility. In that case, $J = 5$. Note that although these five factors are fairly standard, their exact definitions are not standard. Different people use different, though usually correlated, definitions.

Equation 5.2 provides exactly the decomposition shown in Exhibit 5.5. The $\{\beta_j\}$ estimates are all static exposures—that is, they do not vary over time. What we call "pure alpha" in this decomposition is actually the residual in Equation 5.2: the part of the active return that static exposures to smart beta factors cannot explain.

I further decompose the pure alpha return into the general categories shown in Exhibit 5.5:

- Bottom-up security selection, beyond smart beta

- Top-down macro, country, and industry selection, beyond smart beta

- Smart beta timing (i.e., non-static exposures to smart beta factors)

We can easily see how to apply this decomposition to any investment product given the product benchmark and a set of smart beta factor returns. Moreover, we can apply it to several standard categories of investments, as shown in **Exhibits 5.6, 5.7,** and **5.8.**

Exhibit 5.6 shows that index fund returns all come from the cap-weighted index benchmark return. That makes sense, because index funds aim to deliver zero active return.

Exhibit 5.7 shows that smart beta products deliver the cap-weighted index benchmark return *plus* the active return achievable through static exposures to smart beta factors. These products deliver smart beta active returns but not pure alpha returns.

Exhibit 5.8 shows that active management in principle can deliver returns from all these components: the benchmark, smart beta factors, and pure alpha.

As it turns out, active managers vary in how much of each component they attempt to deliver. **Exhibit 5.9** shows the results of the empirical analysis in Kahn and Lemmon (2016) of all the active international equity managers in the eVestment database with data available for the three-year period from April 2011 through March 2014.

Exhibit 5.6.   Index Fund Decomposition

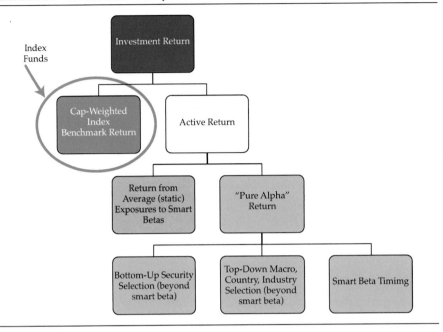

Exhibit 5.7.   Smart Beta Fund Decomposition

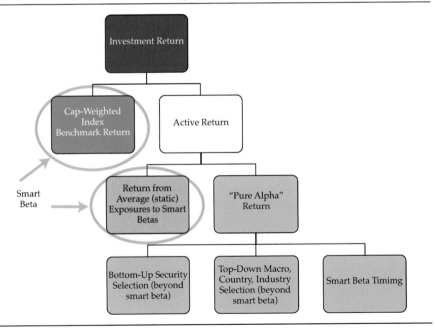

Exhibit 5.8. Active Fund Decomposition

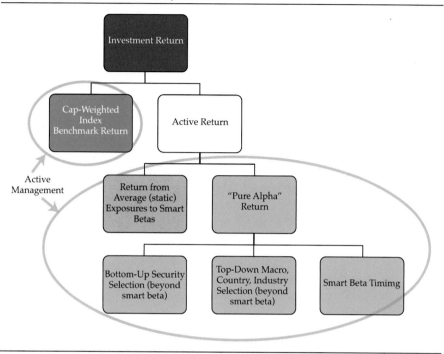

Exhibit 5.9. Distribution of Smart Beta Delivered by Active Managers

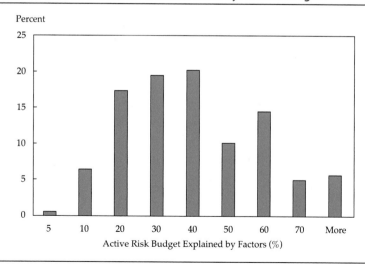

Note: 138 international equity managers; mean equals 35%.
Source: Kahn and Lemmon (2015).

In this case, we regressed the active returns for each of the 138 managers against the Fama–French–Carhart four-factor (market, small size, value, and momentum) model. Exhibit 5.9 shows the distribution of the fraction of active risk represented by those four factors.[52] The distribution is clearly quite broad. On the one hand, there are some active managers—about 25%—who mainly deliver pure alpha. Smart beta factors represent 20% or less of their active risk. On the other hand, another 25% of the managers mainly deliver smart beta, which represents 60% or more of their active risk. This particular example—using international active equity managers and the international Fama–French–Carhart factors—may underestimate the fraction of active risk in smart beta factors, for example, for US equity managers or the managers in just one country. The international factors may explain less risk overall in a multinational setting.

Nothing is wrong with an active manager delivering smart beta. Investors just need to understand what they are buying and pay a fair price for it. Investors shouldn't pay active fees for smart beta. **Exhibit 5.10** shows fee levels as a function of the fraction of active risk in smart beta factors.

The products with the highest fraction of smart beta do seem to be charging reasonable fees, at least at the time of analysis. Exhibit 5.10 highlights the active funds most likely to face disruption. These funds deliver a significant amount of smart beta but charge active fees. I return to the issue of fees in the Trend 7 section.

Smart beta has long been a part of active management, even if some active managers rely very little on it. It turns out that smart beta has also been a significant component of successful active management. Eduard Van Gelderen and Joop Huij (2014) looked at US equity mutual fund performance over the 21-year period from 1990 through 2010. They first calculated fund alphas by regressing fund returns against the CRSP value-weighted index to represent the market. After they eliminated funds with an R^2 less than 60% and funds with less than 36 months of consecutive monthly returns, their study covered 4,026 funds.

Van Gelderen and Huij (2014) separately regressed returns for each of those funds against the larger Fama–French–Carhart set of six factors to determine static exposures to small cap, value, momentum, low volatility (specifically low market beta), short reversal, and long reversal. They classified funds as using particular factors if their regression coefficients were "economically significant," which they characterized as being larger than 0.25, except for low market beta,

---

[52]The fraction of active risk (active variance to be precise) for each fund equals the R^2 statistic from regressing the fund's active returns against the Fama-French-Carhart factor returns.

Exhibit 5.10. Fees vs. Fraction of Smart Beta Delivered

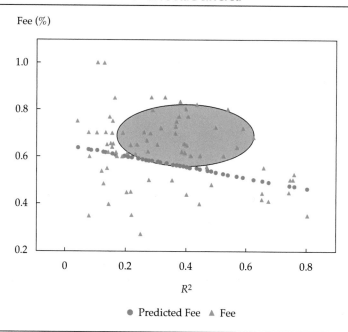

Source: Kahn and Lemmon (2016).

which they characterized as being below 0.8.[53] Finally, they looked at the average alpha by classification. **Exhibit 5.11** displays their results.

If a fund had an economically significant exposure to small cap or value, its probability of positive alpha significantly exceeded 50%. For funds with no economically significant exposures to any smart beta factors, only 20% delivered positive alpha. Historically, smart beta significantly contributed to successful active management.

What about the pure alpha component of active return? As we have seen from the decomposition of active returns, *only* active managers can deliver pure alpha. Investors need all the returns they can get—whether from smart beta or pure alpha. Delivering pure alpha returns must be a key focus of active managers going forward.

How can active managers deliver pure alpha? Early in this chapter, I discussed various reasons to believe successful active management is possible. Excess volatility didn't point to any specific strategies. The arbitrage pricing

---

[53]They discussed several different methods of defining significant exposures. Their results were not very dependent on the choice of method.

Exhibit 5.11. Smart Beta and Successful Active Management

Economically Significant Factor Exposure	Fraction with Positive Alpha
None	20%
Low beta	47
Small cap	61
Value	66
Momentum	37
Short reversal	4
Long reversal	32

Source: Van Gelderen and Huij (2014).

theory underlies smart beta factors. Behavioral finance arguably also underlies some smart beta factors, although it could be a source of pure alpha ideas as well. Investor constraints underlie at least the low-volatility smart beta factor, although they could also lead to pure alpha ideas. Opportunistic trading provides pure alpha but only episodically. The clearest and most promising sources of pure alpha are ideas that involve informational inefficiencies—processing publicly available information faster than the market. If smart beta factors are broad and persistent, pure alpha returns come from more narrow and transient ideas. This is the area where big data and machine learning can significantly contribute.

Success in pure alpha will require strong research capabilities because many pure alpha ideas will last only until the market understands them. Continuous generation of new ideas is critical for long-term success. Success in pure alpha will also require financial engineering skills to hedge out smart beta exposures. Of course, the fundamental law still applies. We need some winning combination of skill, breadth, and efficiency.

I do expect continued investment flows into smart beta/factor products. So far, the growth in smart beta/factor products has mainly been an equity story. Fixed-income smart beta/factor products are still in the early stages of growth. As noted in FTSE Russell *Insights* (June 2017, p. 1), reporting on their global smart beta survey of institutional asset owners, "The trend observed over the past three years of increasing global growth and adoption of smart beta indexes continues in 2017 … It is clearly not a fad, but now widely recognized as a meaningful set of new tools."

Trend 6. Investing Beyond Returns

In tracing investment management from its early history through its intellectual advances in the 20th century and even its current trends, the goal of investment management has always been to deliver returns while controlling risk. Stated more technically, the utility function of investing has included only terms involving expected return and risk.

Although this focus has seemed natural in the context of investment management, it involves a level of precision beyond the economic definition we learned in Econ 101. Economists define utility as a measure of usefulness or satisfaction associated with a good or service, something we can't measure objectively. Financial economists and investment managers, however, have long focused solely on return and risk. This approach has been very fruitful: Look at all the intellectual advances in this field I have discussed. But it may not fully capture what satisfies investors.

In the 1950s and 1960s, labor union pension plans invested in affordable housing projects and health facilities, in part to further social goals. This trend was followed in the 1970s with a broad social movement aimed at forcing university endowments to divest from companies that did business in apartheid-era South Africa, where the majority of the population lived in conditions antithetical to the ideals of those universities. I believe this was the first broad movement aimed at divestiture, although I may be influenced by the daily protests I saw on this topic when I was an undergraduate at Princeton University. As Andrew Rudd commented in his 1979 *Journal of Portfolio Management* article, "Many serious ethical questions are raised by these actions; for instance, to what degree and in which form should the trustees be accountable to the conflicting interests of the fund's beneficiaries." Should university endowments single-mindedly focus on delivering returns, or should they consider other moral and ethical considerations?

The debate over South Africa divestiture pitted return objectives against moral and ethical considerations. The return implications of divestiture appeared significant; they involved 116 companies in the S&P 500, concentrated in a few industries, including business machines, oil, pharmaceuticals, and autos.[54] Excluding more than 100 companies out of the 500 in the S&P 500 and substantially excluding certain large industries seems like it would significantly impair investing in US large-cap stocks. Rudd (1979) examined how well a fund could track the S&P 500 after excluding those

---

[54]See Rudd (1979) for further details. He used a list of US companies doing business in South Africa compiled by the Investor Responsibility Research Center.

116 stocks and found he could reduce the active risk to 2.21%, most of which was stock-specific risk.

The South Africa divestiture movement did have an effect. Hampshire College divested in 1977, and by 1988, 155 college endowments had divested. Divestiture was only one element in raising awareness about the battle against apartheid; the global fallout from the end of the Cold War was the much more direct cause of its actual downfall. The South African government freed Nelson Mandela and other political prisoners in 1990 and dismantled apartheid.

Following the South Africa divestiture movement, socially responsible investing started becoming increasingly popular, with a variety of additional criteria for exclusion, including sin stocks (liquor, tobacco, war-related stocks), nuclear power stocks, and nonunion company stocks (e.g., textile company J.P. Stevens). Some criteria for inclusion also appeared—for example, including stocks of companies recognized for having environmentally sound policies and good customer and employee relations. Rudd (1981) and Hamilton, Jo, and Statman (1993) provided good overviews.

The tobacco divestiture effort of the 1990s is particularly interesting, because it attempted to shift the discussion from a moral/ethical choice to a decision solely about return and risk. I discussed this issue in detail in my 1997 article with Claes Lekander and Tom Leimkuhler.[55] Against a backdrop of increasing numbers of lawsuits against tobacco companies, including state and city lawsuits to recover tobacco-related health care expenses, divestiture advocates used some of the following arguments:

- Maryland state comptroller Louis L. Goldstein stated he was "concerned about the potentially negative long-term impact of litigation on the investment value of U.S. tobacco companies" (p. 63).

- New York State officials claimed they restricted tobacco stock holdings strictly for financial reasons.

- A San Francisco resolution stated the "tobacco stocks can no longer be justified as a prudent investment" (p. 63).

These may be useful arguments for pension plan sponsors trying to balance moral and ethical views with the requirement of investment to meet obligations to beneficiaries. Unfortunately, these investment-based arguments do not hold up to scrutiny. Declaring that tobacco stocks have negative expected returns on the basis of widely publicized lawsuits sounds like active management by public

---

[55]Kahn, Lekander, and Leimkuhler (1997).

officials. Why should that work? Active management can work if it is based on information the market doesn't know or appreciate, but the lawsuits at that time were the most salient facts known about these stocks. I do remember talking to one public pension plan investor who said their informational advantage was in assessing the probability of success of those lawsuits, but he didn't think that was a very compelling argument. It would certainly be reasonable, at least to me, for pension plans to not invest in tobacco because it was killing the beneficiaries, but that wasn't the argument at that time.

Since then, interest in additional criteria for investing has grown in both size and sophistication. Exclusionary screens on tobacco, weapons, and fossil fuels are still popular. On the more sophisticated front, we have seen growth in investing based on environmental, social, and governance (ESG) factors as well as the emergence of *impact investing*, which targets measurable outcomes across such social and environmental goals as alternative energy, health, and inclusion. Sometimes this general approach is referred to as *sustainable investing*. One measure of the increasing sophistication is the movement beyond simple exclusionary rules for portfolio construction. Investors can now measure companies on a continuous scale from good to bad along many dimensions and size their portfolio positions accordingly.

For some sustainable investors, this effort is all or mainly about return and risk—at least over the long term. It may bear some similarity to those state pension plans I discussed that excluded tobacco stocks. For other investors, it goes beyond return and risk to additional components of their utility. I consider sustainable investing expansively as *investing beyond returns*.

One interesting development has been increasing interest in better ways to measure ESG criteria. Of course, it is easy to identify tobacco companies or firearms manufacturers, despite some companies' efforts to diversify or change names. It is more difficult to measure how companies are treating their employees or local communities or how their products are positively affecting the world, beyond company-provided metrics. Some firms that provide ESG metrics make extensive use of the existence of particular company policies as a measure of ESG performance. The big data explosion has helped in this area as well, providing more independent measures of ESG criteria.

What about the size of sustainable investing? The large amount of assets sustainably invested speaks directly to "investing beyond returns" as a key trend for investment management. **Exhibit 5.12** shows the regional breakdown of global sustainable assets (exclusionary screens, ESG, and impact investment strategies) according to the Global Sustainable Investment Alliance (2016).

Total global sustainable assets were a substantial $23 trillion as of 2016. Exhibit 5.12 shows that Europe leads the market in sustainable assets,

Exhibit 5.12. Global Sustainable Assets

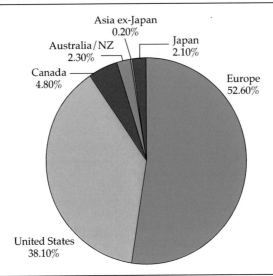

Source: Global Sustainable Investment Alliance (2016).

followed by the United States. The United States is the fastest-growing sustainable market, experiencing almost 24% average annual growth from 2012 through 2016. Consistent with these data, my group at BlackRock finds that every European client and prospect wants to discuss what we are doing in this area, and this topic arises in some of those meetings in the United States and few meetings in Asia, at least so far.

As one more piece of evidence on increasing interest, **Exhibit 5.13** shows the Google Trends analysis of searches on "ESG investing" globally.

Here, too, we see a significant rise in interest, especially from about 2013 through today.

In a similar vein, my group at BlackRock examined the frequency of mentions of the word "diversity" in analyst reports on individual stocks. Analyst reports are not the most obvious place to look for increased interest in ESG investing, but even here, as shown in **Exhibit 5.14**, an increase in mentions of diversity occurred, especially since the global financial crisis. Of course, the term "diversity" is somewhat ambiguous, and Exhibit 5.14 may partly demonstrate an increased interest in diversity of product markets or regional suppliers in the period since the financial crisis, in addition to a diversity of backgrounds among employees. As mentioned earlier in this chapter, text analysis quickly confronts ambiguities.

Exhibit 5.13.   Trend in Global Searches on "ESG Investing"

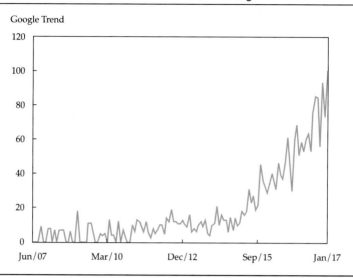

Note: Peak search volume scaled to 100.

Exhibit 5.14.   Analyst Mentions of "Diversity" over Time

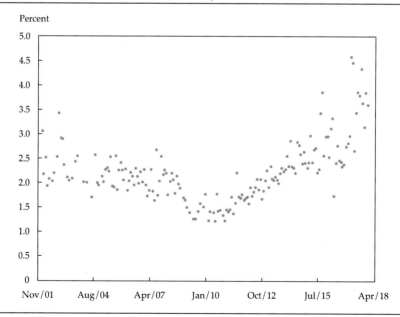

Note: Mentions per month scaled by number of analyst reports per month.
Source: BlackRock.

99

As with any observed trend, we need to ask what caused it and why it should continue. There are a variety of causes for increased sustainable investing, including the following:

- Demographic shifts transferring more control of wealth to women and millennials, two significant groups with high levels of interest in sustainability

- Increased understanding of the risks associated with climate change

- Government regulations increasing company disclosures and, in some cases, requiring that investment managers take sustainability into account

These causes look more likely to intensify than to abate over the next 5–10 years.

Trend 7. Fee Compression

Two of the previous trends—active to passive and smart beta—point toward declining fees for investment management. Index fund fees are far below active fees, and the disruptive innovation of smart beta/factor products was to take standard components of active management, carve them out into transparent rule-based products, and sell them more cheaply than active products. We already know from those trends that investment flows are moving from higher-priced to lower-priced products.

It turns out that those effects do not fully explain the fee compression we have experienced in investment management. Let's explore this trend in more detail.

Consider **Exhibit 5.15**, which shows the trend in expense ratios for active and index mutual funds from 2000 through 2017.

We are focusing on US mutual fund data, as usual, because they are clean, available, and public and they appear to be consistent with the broader industry trend.

Exhibit 5.15 displays asset-weighted averages. They have been falling for equity and bond funds and for active and index funds over this 18-year period. Even within each category, fees have compressed.

To further see the relative importance of flows to lower-fee products and product fees compressing, consider that, also according to the Investment Company Institute (2018), the overall equity mutual fund asset-weighted expense ratio was 0.99% in 2000 and 0.59% in 2017, whereas the overall bond mutual fund asset-weighted expense ratio was 0.76% in 2000 and 0.48% in 2017. The overall asset-weighted expense ratio in each asset class is simply the weighted average of the asset-weighted average active and index fund fees.

Exhibit 5.15. **Expense Ratios of Actively Managed and Index Mutual Funds**

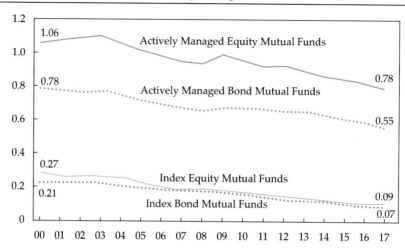

Source: Investment Company Institute (2018).

For example,

$$\text{Fee}_{equity} = w \cdot \text{Fee}_{active\ equity} + (1-w) \cdot \text{Fee}_{index\ equity}. \tag{5.3}$$

Here, we ignore the smart beta/factor products because the data do not break out that category. Doing so shouldn't dramatically change the results because smart beta/factor products have mainly been an equity phenomenon so far and flows to them have mainly occurred over the past few years. Using Equation 5.3 and the average fee numbers already mentioned, we can estimate the percentage of assets invested in active products (the term w in Equation 5.3). **Exhibit 5.16** shows the results.

Exhibit 5.16 agrees with the intuition that indexing has increased over time and plays a bigger role in equity investing. If we saw this increase in indexing percentage without any change in fees for active and indexing

Exhibit 5.16. **Implied Active and Index Weights**

	% of Assets in Active	
	2000	2017
Equity	91.1%	72.5%
Bond	96.5	85.4

products, it would lead to average equity fees dropping from 0.99% to 0.84% and average bond fees dropping from 0.76% to 0.70%. Thus, the shift in assets from active to index, by itself, explains less than half of the total drop in fees.

Why have asset-weighted expense ratios of active and index, equity and bond mutual funds been dropping? There are at least three reasons. First, assets have been flowing into the lowest-fee funds in each category. About 75% of the assets are invested in funds in the bottom 25% of fees, as of 2017. Lower-cost funds attract most of the assets. Second, individual fund fees have been falling. We can see this clearly in the world of index funds. For example, fees have steadily dropped for S&P 500 Index ETFs over the past few years. The iShares S&P 500 ETF cost 0.09% in 2011, 0.07% in 2012, and 0.04% in 2016. The Vanguard S&P 500 ETF cost 0.05% in 2011 and 0.04% since 2017. Retail investors can access broad market index ETFs for less than 5 bps, and institutional investors pay even less. The third reason that fees are compressing within category is that new funds launch with lower fees. For example, my group at BlackRock recently launched a series of equity mutual funds with below-average fees for active equity funds.

Can fee compression continue? Assets can still flow from active to index and smart beta/factor products, lowering average fees. As for individual product fees, on the index fund side there is not much more room to drop. The fees for broad and liquid indexes, such as the S&P 500, are already below 5 bps. These funds incur costs to run, including portfolio management, legal, and distribution expenses. The institutions offering these funds also assume some risk of operating errors, the cost of which scales with asset size. We shouldn't expect index fees to drop to zero, and hence, they probably have little additional room to fall. That said, as I am completing this book in August 2018, Fidelity Investments just announced two broad equity index funds with zero fees.

What about active management fees? Let's focus on pure alpha fees because smart beta/factor funds are quickly lowering fees for those strategies. My group at BlackRock thinks about fees as a fraction of alpha delivered. If we deliver a certain amount of alpha, how much goes to the investor (the asset owner) and how much goes to us? This breakdown is explicit for hedge funds, which typically charge a 2% base fee plus 20% of the positive alpha delivered. To be clear, they receive 20% of the alpha delivered if it is positive. Negative delivered alpha does not reduce their fee. Between the 2% base fee and the incentive fee paid only for positive delivered alpha, hedge funds keep more than 20% of the alpha they deliver.

We can think about fixed fees in the same way, representing a fraction of the expected alpha. The fraction should fall somewhere between 20% and

35%, with higher fractions going to funds with higher information ratios. Such funds deliver more consistent alpha, and investors likely have more confidence that they have identified a skillful manager. More capacity-constrained products and niche products also tend to demand high-fractional shares.

As a general comment, it is expensive to produce consistent pure alpha return streams—between the costs of the required data and the costs of the required talented individuals, who are often highly sought out by investment management competitors and, for big data and machine learning experts, technology firms.

What does the 20%–35% sharing range tell us about mutual fund fees, which are a fixed percentage of assets? We already saw that the average mutual fund subtracted alpha, so this analysis will not work when applied to aggregate delivered alpha. Instead, consider the following "hand-waving" analysis. Let's assume that investors choose active funds they believe will deliver top-quartile performance. (If you think we should focus on the top 15th percentile or 30th percentile, that's beyond the precision of this analysis.) Let's look at average mutual fund fees and compare them with the 20%–35% sharing range.

I estimate top-quartile performance as follows. As discussed in Chapter 4, a top-quartile mutual fund information ratio before fees is about 0.5. If we multiply that by the typical active risk level, we can estimate a top-quartile active return. To estimate typical active risk levels for mutual funds, BlackRock used the Morningstar database of mutual fund returns over the period from October 1997 through September 2017 and divided those data into four five-year periods to better understand how active risk varies over time. We calculated the median realized active risk for large-cap US equity funds and for US broad fixed-income funds. The median US large-cap equity mutual fund active risk varied from a high of 7.75% in the earliest period to a low of 3.18% in the most recent period. For the broad US fixed-income mutual funds, the median active risk varied from a high of 2.81% during the five-year period containing the global financial crisis (October 2007–September 2012) to a low of 0.85% during the previous period (October 2002–September 2007). Averaging the median active risk numbers over these four periods, we found 4.79% active risk for US large-cap funds and 1.45% for broad US fixed-income funds.

Based on the averages over those four periods, we expect a top-quartile US active equity manager to deliver about 2.4% active return before fees. Our sharing range implies that fees should range between about 84 bps and

48 bps. The average expense ratio is currently 78 bps—near the top of the range—so there may be a little more room for equity fund fees to fall.

For bond mutual funds, we expect a top-quartile manager to deliver about 0.72% active return before fees.[56] The same sharing range implies that fees should range between 25 bps and 14 bps. Because the average expense ratio is currently 55 bps, there appears to be more room for bond fund fees to fall, which will be challenging because the costs of managing an active bond fund aren't much different from the costs of managing an active equity fund. I first wrote about this phenomenon in "Bond Managers Need to Take More Risk" in 1998, where I pointed out the mismatch between active risk and fees for bond funds. It's still an issue in 2018.

Investment management fees have compressed over the past two decades, and that trend may well continue. Furthermore, incentive fees may become more prevalent. They represent fees as a percentage of alpha delivered, which is the natural way to think about fees. They also align the incentives of the manager with the investor, though not perfectly, as discussed in Kahn, Scanlan, and Siegel (2006).

Bibliography

Barras, Laurent, Olivier Scaillet, and Russ Wermers. 2010. "False Discoveries in Mutual Fund Performance: Measuring Luck in Estimated Alphas." *Journal of Finance* 65 (1): 179–216.

Benz, Christine. 2008. "Bogle on a Knock against Indexing." Morningstar video interview (23 September). www.morningstar.com/cover/VideoCenter.aspx?id=255347.

Burning Glass, IBM, and the Business-Higher Education Forum. 2017. "The Quant Crunch: How the Demand for Data Science Skills Is Disrupting the Job Market." https://www.burning-glass.com/wp-content/uploads/The_Quant_Crunch.pdf.

Butler, Declan. 2013. "When Google Got Flu Wrong." *Nature* 494: 155–6.

Carhart, Mark M. 1997. "On Persistence in Mutual Fund Performance." *Journal of Finance* 52 (1): 57–82.

Fama, Eugene F., and Kenneth R. French. 1992. "The Cross-Section of Expected Stock Returns." *Journal of Finance*, 47 (2): 427–65.

---

[56]Top-quartile information ratios for fixed income may be a bit higher because of some structural issues around the construction of fixed-income indexes that provide opportunities to outperform them.

————. French. 2010. "Luck versus Skill in the Cross Section of Mutual Fund Returns." *Journal of Finance*, 65 (5): 1915–47.

French, Kenneth R. 2008. "The Cost of Active Investing." *Journal of Finance* 63 (4): 1537–73.

Ginsberg, Jeremy, Matthew H. Mohebbi, Rajan S. Patel, Lynnette Brammer, Mark S. Smolinski, and Larry Brilliant. 2009. "Detecting Influenza Epidemics Using Search Engine Query Data." *Science* 457: 1012–14.

Global Sustainable Investment Alliance. 2016. "Global Sustainable Investment Review." www.gsi-alliance.org/wp-content/uploads/2017/03/GSIR_Review2016.F.pdf.

Grinold, Richard C., and Ronald N. Kahn. 2000. *Active Portfolio Management*, 2nd ed. New York: McGraw-Hill.

Grossman, Sanford J., and Joseph E. Stiglitz. 1980. "On the Impossibility of Informationally Efficient Markets." *American Economic Review* 70 (3): 393–408.

Hamilton, Sally, Hoje Jo, and Meir Statman. 1993. "Doing Well by Doing Good? The Investment Performance of Socially Responsible Mutual Funds." *Financial Analysts Journal* (November/December): 62–66.

Huij, Joop, and Simon Lansdorp. 2012. "Mutual Fund Performance Persistence, Market Efficiency, and Breadth." Working paper (25 October).

Investment Company Institute. 2018. "Investment Company Fact Book: 2018." www.ici.org/pdf/2018_factbook.pdf.

Kahn, Ronald N. 1998. "Bond Managers Need to Take More Risk." *Journal of Portfolio Management* (Spring): 70–76.

Kahn, Ronald N., Claes Lekander, and Tom Leimkuhler. 1997. "Just Say No? The Investment Implications of Tobacco Divestiture." *Journal of Investing* (Winter): 62–70.

Kahn, Ronald N., and Michael Lemmon. 2015. "Smart Beta: The Owner's Manual." *Journal of Portfolio Management* (Winter): 76–83.

Kahn, Ronald N., and Michael Lemmon. 2016. "The Asset Manager's Dilemma: How Smart Beta Is Disrupting the Investment Management Industry." *Financial Analysts Journal* 72 (1): 15–20.

Kahn, Ronald N., and Andrew Rudd. 1995. "Does Historical Performance Predict Future Performance?" *Financial Analysts Journal* (November/December): 43–52.

Kahn, Ronald N., Matthew H. Scanlan, and Laurence B. Siegel. 2006. "Five Myths about Fees." *Journal of Portfolio Management* (Spring): 56–64.

Kaplan, Steve, and Antoinette Schoar. 2005. "Private Equity Performance: Returns, Persistence, and Capital Flows." *Journal of Finance* 60 (4):1791–823.

McLean, R. David, and Jeffrey Pontiff. 2016. "Does Academic Research Destroy Stock Return Predictability?" *Journal of Finance* 71 (1): 5–32.

Ross, Stephen A. 1976. "The Arbitrage Theory of Capital Asset Pricing." *Journal of Economic Theory* 13 (3): 341–60.

Rudd, Andrew. 1979. "Divestment of South African Equities: How Risky?" *Journal of Portfolio Management* 5 (3): 5–10.

———. 1981. "Social Responsibility and Portfolio Performance." *California Management Review* (Summer): 55–61.

Thompson, Jennifer. 2017. "Smart Beta Funds Pass $1tn in Assets." *Financial Times* (27 December).

"Trends and Outlook for Smart Beta." 2017. *FTSE Russell Insights* (June).

Van Gelderen, Eduard, and Joop Huij. 2014. "Academic Knowledge Dissemination in the Mutual Fund Industry: Can Mutual Funds Successfully Adopt Factor Investing Strategies?" *Journal of Portfolio Management* (Summer): 157–67.

6. The Future of Investment Management

The future is no longer what it used to be.

—*Friedrich Hollander*

We have now studied the modern history of investment management—the origins of the field and the development of its key ideas. I have provided several important insights into active management, including the arithmetic of active management and the fundamental law of active management. And I have discussed seven trends that will help predict the future of investment management, at least over the next 5–10 years.

In the 1960s, investment management was active management. Investment management is now evolving into three branches:

- Indexing

- Smart beta/factor investing

- Pure alpha investing

The indexing branch is already clear and distinct, even though it may continue to evolve. The smart beta/factor investing branch has developed more recently, and I expect it to grow. The pure alpha branch of investment management is less well defined today and has evolved as the part of active management complementary to smart beta/factor investing.

These three branches will each offer two styles of products: those that focus exclusively on returns and those that also include goals beyond returns.

I discuss each of these branches and styles in turn, considering the underlying investment case, the requirements for investment and business success, and what could go wrong. Let's start with indexing.

Index Funds

Index funds have existed for almost 50 years now, and they are more popular than ever. As discussed in Chapter 5, money has been steadily flowing from active to index funds over the past decade. Even if that trend eases, indexing is already a significant, established branch of investing. Perhaps the most certain statement we can make about the future of investment management is that indexing will be a significant part of it.

The investment case for indexing is compelling. Both the CAPM and the EMH argue for index funds. Even if there are consistently successful active managers, Sharpe's arithmetic of active management states that the average active manager will underperform, and the empirical evidence all supports that statement. Furthermore, indexing is the one area of investment management that can consistently deliver on its promises. The large S&P 500 Index funds consistently deliver the S&P 500 return minus a very small management fee day after day, year after year.

My former colleague Barton Waring and his co-author, Laurence Siegel, said in their 2003 *Journal of Portfolio Management* article that there are two requirements for an investor to choose active management:

- The investor must believe superior active managers exist.

- The investor must have the skill to identify the active managers who will deliver positive active returns in the future.

If investors follow this thoughtful advice, many will choose indexing. For most institutional investors and for increasing numbers of retail investors, the question is no longer whether to invest in index funds but, rather, how much to allocate to index funds relative to active funds.

Index funds have also benefited from strong investor interest in exchange-traded funds. The majority of ETFs are index funds, though not necessarily broad market index funds as envisioned in the academic arguments in favor of indexing. Exchange-traded funds offer some distinct advantages over other fund structures, including continuous pricing and liquidity—investors can trade them throughout the day—and tax efficiency. The continuing interest in ETFs also supports the case that indexing will be a significant component of investment management going forward.

Successful indexing is all about delivering index exposure as reliably and cheaply as possible. The demands for closely and reliably tracking indexes require strong financial engineering skills and technology. The ability to offer exposures cheaply requires scale. The most successful indexing firms are incredibly large in terms of assets under management, and we expect index fund management to consolidate for scale. That has largely already happened. These firms offer very low fee index funds.

Many things could go wrong in investment management, but nothing would systemically threaten indexing as an important category. An extended period of low or negative returns could shift some assets out of indexing and into active management, but the arguments in favor of indexing are too strong for that situation to eliminate indexing as an investment management category. A particular fund offered by a particular manager might suffer a crippling operating error, but that would threaten only that fund and that manager. Indexing does not seem to face systemic risks.

Smart Beta/Factor Funds

Smart beta/factor products are recent developments in investment management. As I discussed, the underlying investment ideas are anything but recent developments; most have been around for decades, if not centuries. The packaging of these ideas into products is the big innovation.

The investment case for smart beta/factor products is strong, although not as strong as the case for indexing. Whereas the arithmetic of active management essentially guarantees that broad market index funds will be consistent above-median performers, smart beta/factor funds might be top-quartile performers, on average, but could deliver bottom-quartile performance in certain years.

Because these products resemble index funds in their transparency, rule-based approach to implementation, and low cost, they benefit to some extent from investor interest in index funds. Similarly, many smart beta products are ETFs and thus benefit from the general investor interest in those vehicles.

The requirements for investment and business success in smart beta/factor products closely resemble the requirements for success in indexing. Once again, it is all about delivering exposure to factors as reliably and cheaply as possible, with the associated advantages to scale. This field is more recent than indexing, and many firms offer these products. I expect consolidation over time, such that a small number of firms will manage most of the smart beta/factor assets. Smart beta/factor fees are lower than active management fees, and they have been falling.

This is a new area of investment management, and at least three things could go wrong that would systemically threaten the category. First, smart beta/factor products could go through an extended period of underperformance. As previously noted, there is no guarantee that these factors will outperform every year. Even multi-factor products that benefit from the diversification across factors cannot guarantee that they will consistently outperform.

In traditional active management and in pure alpha management, performance depends on the manager. If a manager underperforms over an extended period, investors will fire her. That could also cause those investors to question active management generally, but if they invest across several active managers, they will probably observe some that are succeeding.

Smart beta/factor products are different in that managers are delivering exposures to factors that investors want. Do you fire the manager if the smart beta product underperforms? Would you fire the index fund manager if the index underperforms? Extended underperformance of a given smart beta category could cause investors to question the category more than the manager. Thus, smart beta underperformance may systemically threaten this entire branch of investment management in a way that active manager underperformance doesn't threaten active management. That said, given the diversity of smart beta factors and their performance across regions, it is unlikely that most or all smart beta/factor products would underperform in the same period.

The second thing that could go wrong with smart beta/factor investing is somewhat related to the first. Both concern underperformance. This second potential landmine, however, is significant short-term underperformance that could arise after the buildup of many large and correlated smart beta/factor funds. Sudden and substantial outflows from those funds, possibly in response to events unrelated to smart beta/factors, could generate sizable short-term underperformance. This happened to quantitative equity strategies, particularly a short-term trading strategy called statistical arbitrage but also what we now call smart beta factors—value, momentum, small size, and quality—in early August 2007. Huge amounts of money had flowed into these funds in the prior few years. Some investors treated these funds almost like money market funds—highly liquid with appealing information ratios. When the subprime mortgage crisis triggered margin calls at firms with illiquid subprime mortgage holdings, several of those firms simultaneously started selling their more liquid quantitative equity funds to raise cash. Too many funds exiting at the same time led to extreme negative returns in the seemingly diversified equity funds, and several highly leveraged quantitative equity hedge funds folded. About 75% of the assets invested in quantitative equity funds left over the following two to three years. A sudden and significant drawdown, correlated across many smart beta/factor products, could also systemically threaten this emerging branch of investment management.

The third thing that could go wrong concerns the still-developing investor understanding of smart beta/factor investing. In particular, investors may not understand how performance can significantly vary from one product to the next. In the world of index funds, investors do understand that the performance of an S&P 500 Index fund will differ from the performance of a Russell 1000 Index fund, and they even understand the most likely source of that difference: the presence of some smaller stocks in the Russell 1000.

Investors do not have that level of understanding of smart beta/factor funds. Two funds can both invest in "value" or "low volatility," but those characteristics are not precisely defined. Different funds will use different definitions, and sometimes those different definitions will lead to significantly differing performance. In most of those cases, both choices are reasonable *ex ante*; they just vary in performance *ex post*. Investor experience with divergent performance could sour them on smart beta/factor products as a category.

Pure Alpha Funds

The third branch of investment management consists of the pure alpha funds. I believe that as smart beta/factor funds establish themselves and offer components of traditional active management cheaply, active managers will need to focus on delivering the part of active returns that investors can't access through smart beta/factor funds.

Pure alpha investing faces the most difficult investment case. We expect most pure alpha products to underperform on the basis of the arithmetic of active management. That said, there are reasons to believe that some pure alpha managers can succeed, based on informational inefficiencies, behavioral anomalies, investor constraints, and some opportunistic trades. The top pure alpha investors should be able to deliver consistent performance.

In this case, the requirements for success are very different from what we saw for indexing and smart beta/factor investing. Pure alpha investing is not about delivering exposures cheaply. Much of it is about finding publicly available information the market doesn't yet understand. Broad and persistent factors are relatively easy to find—exactly because they are broad and persistent.

Pure alpha ideas are narrower and more transient. That transience means that successful pure alpha investing requires constant innovation, hence the strong research capabilities able to drive that innovation. Successful pure alpha investors must constantly replace old ideas that the market now understands with fresh ideas. The new world of big data and machine learning is providing great opportunities for innovation. Quantitative pure alpha investors—especially those who have the required skills—are already exploiting these opportunities. Other pure alpha investors will need to upgrade their skills in this technical area. Pure alpha investing is too difficult for any investor to ignore any opportunities.

For pure alpha investors, the appeal of long–short investing will be especially compelling. I have shown that the long-only constraint has a significant impact on portfolio efficiency and that this impact increases with active risk. Just as pure alpha investors can't afford to ignore big data and machine learning, they also can't afford to ignore the impact of the long-only constraint. I expect that successful pure alpha managers will offer long–short or partial short products in the interest of efficiency. More generally, I expect to see successful pure alpha managers in the private equity and alternative spaces—areas that even today demonstrate relatively convincing evidence of successful active management, as mentioned in Chapter 5.

Pure alpha investing is distinctly not a scale business: It is capacity constrained. It is not an area where I expect consolidation, at least at the fund level. Instead, the most successful pure alpha investment firms will be research-driven boutiques, possibly including some boutiques within larger asset management firms.

Successful pure alpha investing is expensive because of the requirement of constant innovation and its associated demand for highly skilled professionals. Consistent pure alpha performance is quite valuable to investors. In spite of current pressures, I do not expect fees to fall much, especially for the most successful products. Many of these funds use incentive fees that depend on delivered performance and generally—though not completely—align managers and investors.[57]

Although plenty can go wrong with individual pure alpha products, I expect products to be uncorrelated on average. Poor performance will threaten individual funds without also threatening the entire pure active branch of investment management. More than 50 years after the development of the CAPM, index funds have now made significant inroads against active management. But doing so took 50 years, and most assets are still actively managed.

Investing Beyond Returns

As I have discussed, the trend toward investing beyond returns—including ESG factors—shows no sign of abating. Non-investment goals can live side-by-side with investment goals. Grouping those factors under the general heading of *sustainability*, investors will have their choice of sustainable index funds, sustainable smart beta/factor funds, and sustainable pure alpha funds, along with their standard counterparts. These funds already exist. I expect more and more such offerings, including newer funds based on increasingly available independent data that inform our views of companies along many sustainability dimensions.

In these funds, the investment case is built mainly on investor utility beyond returns, although in some instances investors believe these ideas predict long-run returns or help avoid long-run risk. Some of these products—such as those that simply exclude tobacco stocks—are easy to implement, and thus all investment firms should be able to offer products in this area.

To be fair, many investors find these simpler products based on various exclusions to be the most transparent and hence the most compelling. The more sophisticated products—those where portfolio weights depend on a continuous scale of sustainability along multiple dimensions and where

---

[57]Kahn, Scanlan, and Siegel (2006).

independently gathered data inform those sustainability metrics—will require a dedicated research staff devoted to the area. Stated another way: All investment firms can offer products in this area, but only the more sophisticated and research-driven firms can offer state-of-the-art sustainability products.

What could go wrong in the world of investing beyond returns? First, the returns to these products could significantly lag behind their non-sustainability counterparts. Many people have studied this question over time. Meir Statman and Denys Glushkov (2016) examined the performance of US socially responsible mutual funds by defining two distinct new factors, similar to the factors previously proposed by Fama, French, and Carhart:

- TMB (top minus bottom) is a factor that is long stocks in the top third along various socially responsible criteria and short stocks in the bottom third along the same dimensions.

- AMS (accepted minus shunned) is a factor that is long stocks commonly accepted by socially responsible investors and short stocks commonly shunned, including alcohol, tobacco, gaming, firearms, military, and nuclear power stocks.

In short, they found positive returns associated with the TMB factor and negative returns associated with the AMS factor. Every socially responsible fund will have its own exposures to these two factors, but typically they have positive exposures to both. The end result is fairly small and often not statistically significant differences in performance.

In the end, investors like these funds because they align with their beliefs. It would take significant underperformance to deter them. I do not see evidence of a level of underperformance that would threaten this entire approach to investing.

A second thing that could go wrong is mainly a challenge for providers of these funds. Once we move beyond return and risk, views on environmental, social, and governance factors vary widely. I remember being surprised when a church pension plan asked us to exclude Disney—which seemed to me a very wholesome, family-oriented company. The problem was Disney's policy of providing domestic partner benefits for employees, which violated church tenets. I don't bring up this example in any way to question this pension plan's beliefs or sincerity. Rather, it is just one of many examples I have experienced of different investors having specific "beyond returns" views on certain companies. The challenge for investment managers is that the pool of clients—and their viewpoints or beliefs—may be quite disparate. There may not be any one-size-fits-all fund possibilities or even anything close to that. Given the assets in these investments already and the availability of technology to facilitate managing large numbers of separate accounts, this problem does not seem to be insurmountable.

A third thing that could go wrong is a loss of faith in the metrics used to measure sustainability. Garvey, Kazdin, LaFond, Nash, and Safa (2017) showed that, contrary to expectations, high ESG ratings predict, rather than prevent, controversies. The methodologies used to measure ESG ratings are company reported and are often based on companies having particular ESG-related policies. As it turns out, companies often develop such policies in response to circumstances and controversies that predict future controversies. This is not a criticism of sustainable investing but, rather, evidence of the need for better metrics.

Fees

I have already discussed the trend in fee compression and argued that it has little further room to go for index funds and more room to go for active funds, especially bond funds. For bond funds, the issue may be less about fees and more about the mismatch between fees and active risk.

Concerning fees for pure alpha, as we have noted, pure alpha is expensive to produce, valuable for investors, and capacity constrained. Therefore, in spite of fee pressures on active managers, including pure alpha managers, we expect fees on pure alpha products to remain high, especially for the most successful pure alpha managers. We also expect these products to increasingly offer incentive fees. This is the natural way to think about fees—as a fraction of pure alpha delivered—and it generally aligns manager and investor incentives. Investors pay high fees when performance is strong.

Overall, looking forward, we expect low fixed fees and increasing use of incentive fees in investment management.

Conclusion

Over the course of this book, I have traced investment management from its early origins through a set of intellectual developments that have strongly influenced the field today and its likely future development.

Indexing is a significant component of investment management today, and it will remain a significant component. We can trace indexing back to the CAPM and the EMH of the 1960s and to the arithmetic of active management in 1991.

Smart beta/factor investing goes back, in part, to Stephen Ross and arbitrage pricing theory in 1976, as well as to a set of very old investment ideas. We saw evidence of value investing in the Dutch investment trusts of the late

1700s. The ideas may go back even further, but the trail of detailed evidence ends there.

Pure alpha investing builds on the informational inefficiency argument of Grossman and Stiglitz, although it was clearly happening long before they analyzed it. The story of the Rothschilds using carrier pigeons to learn the outcome of the Battle of Waterloo in advance of their competitors and then successfully trading on that knowledge (even if not exactly true)[58] testifies to the long-understood value of finding out material information before others.

Investing beyond returns—sustainable investing, socially responsible investing, ESG investing—is in some ways a slight counterpoint to investment management's increasingly systematic focus on return and risk. It recognizes that utility functions are more complicated and many investors have goals beyond just high returns and low risk. It is not a refutation of the great advances brought by Markowitz but, rather, an acknowledgement that human nature, and thus investment management, is too complicated to reduce to two variables. As we have seen, however, investment management can handle many return factors systematically. It can even handle non-return factors systematically, and there are already funds that combine return and non-return factors transparently, based on models. We have yet to see a widely accepted approach to optimizing a portfolio for multiple objectives, but I expect to see such a development in the next few years.

Investment management is an inherently uncertain activity. Risk—the distribution of potential outcomes—is unavoidable. But the approach to this uncertain activity is increasingly systematic. Indexing and smart beta/factor investing are both very systematic. Pure alpha investing has become increasingly systematic as the understanding has grown for the magnitude of the challenge. Sustainable investing is often quite systematic.

Over the course of its recorded history, from the late 1700s in the Netherlands to a global industry today, investment management has become increasingly systematic. Over that same period but especially since the development of indexing, investment management has become more specialized, offering transparency and low costs where possible. Both of these high-level trends will continue.

Bibliography

Garvey, Gerald T., Joshua Kazdin, Ryan LaFond, Joanna Nash, and Hussein Safa. 2017. "A Pitfall in Ethical Investing: ESG Disclosures Reflect Vulnerabilities, Not Virtues." *Journal of Investment Management* 15 (2): 51–64.

---

[58]John Kay (2013).

Kahn, Ronald N., Matthew H. Scanlan, and Laurence B. Siegel. 2006. "Five Myths about Fees." *Journal of Portfolio Management* 32 (3): 56–64.

Kay, John. 2013. "Enduring Lessons from the Legend of Rothschild's Carrier Pigeon." *Financial Times* (28 May).

Statman, Meir, and Denys Glushkov. 2016. "Classifying and Measuring the Performance of Socially Responsible Mutual Funds." *Journal of Portfolio Management* (Winter): 1–12.

Waring, Barton, and Laurence B. Siegel. 2003. "The Dimensions of Active Management." *Journal of Portfolio Management* 29 (3): 35–51.

Named Endowments

The CFA Institute Research Foundation acknowledges with sincere gratitude the generous contributions of the Named Endowment participants listed below.

Gifts of at least US$100,000 qualify donors for membership in the Named Endowment category, which recognizes in perpetuity the commitment toward unbiased, practitioner-oriented, relevant research that these firms and individuals have expressed through their generous support of the CFA Institute Research Foundation.

Senior Research Fellows

Financial Services Analyst Association

For more on upcoming Research Foundation
publications and webcasts, please visit
www.cfainstitute.org/learning/foundation.

Research Foundation monographs
are online at www.cfapubs.org.

RESEARCH FOUNDATION
CONTRIBUTION FORM

☑ **Yes**, I want the Research Foundation to continue to fund innovative research that advances the investment management profession. Please accept my tax-deductible contribution at the following level:

Thought Leadership Circle..................... US$1,000,000 or more
Named Endowment...................... US$100,000 to US$999,999
Research Fellow .... US$10,000 to US$99,999
Contributing Donor............................US$1,000 to US$9,999
Friend .... Up to US$999

I would like to donate US$ _____.

☐ My check is enclosed (payable to the CFA Institute Research Foundation).
☐ I would like to donate appreciated securities (send me information).
☐ Please charge my donation to my credit card.
　　　　　　☐ VISA　☐ MC　☐ Amex　☐ Diners

Card Number

____ / ____　　　　　_____
Expiration Date　　　　Name on card　PLEASE PRINT
☐ Corporate Card
☐ Personal Card　　　_____
　　　　　　　　　　　　Signature
☐ This is a pledge. Please bill me for my donation of US$_____
☐ I would like recognition of my donation to be:
　　☐ Individual donation　☐ Corporate donation　☐ Different individual

_____
PLEASE PRINT NAME OR COMPANY NAME AS YOU WOULD LIKE IT TO APPEAR

PLEASE PRINT　☐ Mr.　☐ Mrs.　☐ Ms.　　MEMBER NUMBER _____

_____
Last Name (Family Name)　　　First (Given Name)　　Middle Initial

_____
Title

_____
Address

_____
City　　　　　　　State/Province　　Country ZIP/Postal Code

Please mail this completed form with your contribution to:
The CFA Institute Research Foundation • P.O. Box 2082
Charlottesville, VA 22902-2082 USA

For more on the CFA Institute Research Foundation, please visit www.cfainstitute.org/learning/foundation/Pages/index.aspx.

Made in the USA
Columbia, SC
28 November 2018